7 Steps
from SAD
to Happy

TURNING WINTERTIME BLUES & SEASONAL AFFECTIVE DISORDER INTO A HAPPIER LIFE

by Dr. Jay Polmar

Cover designed by Liliana Gonzalez Garcia,
www.ipublicidades.com

The Saddest Thing in My Personal Life

The saddest thing that I've ever seen, is when the seasons change and my wife's smile disappears, and the waterfalls begin to flow from her eyes. Everything becomes depressing, everything turns from golden to darkness, and she spends her life in bed, crying, watching soap operas, or on Facebook.

For 8 years I have searched for the cure in medication for her, there is none she would take. Then I researched meditation, yoga, music therapy, hypnotherapy, and Lighting.

My suggestion for those who suffer is simply:

☺ **Let the Sun Shine In -**

☺ **Face It With A Grin**

☺ **Open Up Your Heart and**

☺ **Let The Sun Shine In....**

These are the remedies that we found and that worked and at this time, we'd love to share them with you. They do work, with a little bit of time, and cooperation.

7 STEPS
from **SAD** to Happy

TURNING WINTERTIME BLUES & SEASONAL AFFECTIVE DISORDER INTO A

Happier Life

by Dr. Jay Polmar

Table of Contents

It is

so

SAD!

What's SAD?

An Introduction to Seasonal Affective Disorder

SAD is an acronym for Seasonal Affective Disorder. It describes a specific type of depression, which occurs at a certain time of the year, usually in the winter. SAD is triggered by the change of the seasons and reduction of amount of natural sunlight and has recently became an increasingly understood illness with more research being done every year.

SAD sometimes is referred to as winter-onset depression because many of its symptoms usually appear in the late fall or early winter and seem to taper away by summer.

There is, however, another type of SAD that is much less common and less referred to, and that is summer-onset depression in which symptoms appear late spring or early summer and taper off long before winter.

 This book will focus on the most common type which is Winter-Onset SAD as it has been more vetted and more is known about it.

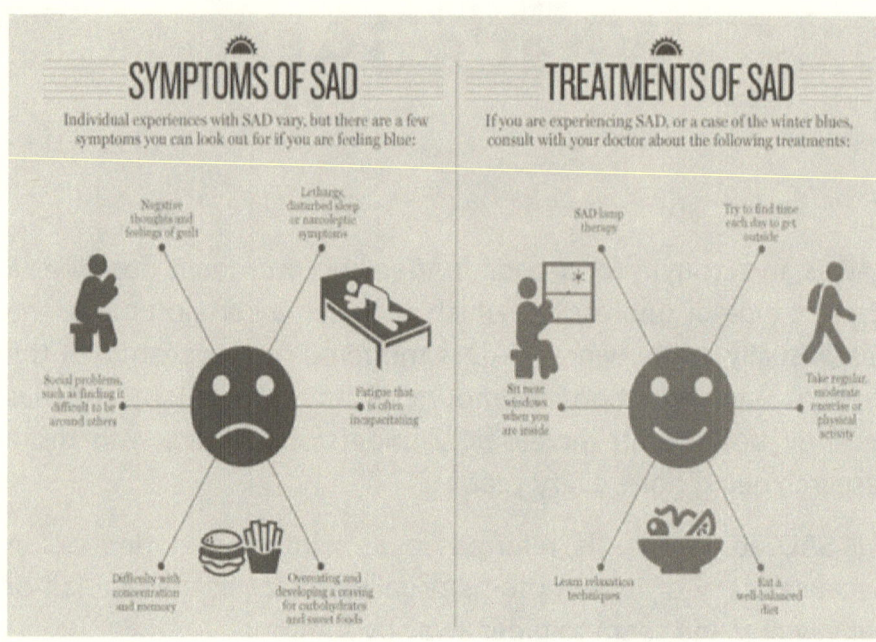

SYMPTOMS OF SAD

Individual experiences with SAD vary, but there are a few symptoms you can look out for if you are feeling blue:

Negative thoughts and feelings of guilt

Lethargy, disturbed sleep or narcoleptic symptoms

Social problems, such as finding it difficult to be around others

Fatigue that is often incapacitating

Difficulty with concentration and memory

Overeating and developing a craving for carbohydrates and sweet foods

TREATMENTS OF SAD

If you are experiencing SAD, or a case of the winter blues, consult with your doctor about the following treatments:

SAD lamp therapy

Try to find time each day to get outside

Sit near windows when you are inside

Take regular, moderate exercise or physical activity

Learn relaxation techniques

Eat a well-balanced diet

Some Facts About SAD 😧

SAD is not uncommon and can be a seriously debilitating condition. It is essential to know about SAD because you or likely someone you know suffers from it.

In fact, it is estimated that between 4% and 6% of all people in the United States suffer from SAD and an additional 10% to 20% may experience SAD symptoms during the winter but do not meet the clinical standards of having the disease.

SAD usually affects people aged 20 or older and while extremely uncommon in children and teenagers is less common in this younger age group. Past the age of fifty, the risk of developing SAD decreases considerably.

SAD is more prevalent in women than in men. It is thought to affect 4x as many women as men.

Factors such as personal biology, brain chemistry, family history, environment, and life experiences all seem to factors in who is at risk for developing SAD.

People living in colder climates where winters are longer and more persistent are at higher risk for developing SAD.

SAD had been recognized, as a health issue, for over 150 years, but it was not until the mid-1980s that it was finally recognized as a mental health disorder; it is now a subset of a category in depression and bi-polar disorder accounting to the approved diagnostic code system used by doctors, the government and insurance companies.

Unfortunately, the exact cause of Seasonal Affective Disorder (SAD) is unknown. The symptoms of depression are believed to be linked with the shorter days of the year. It occurs during the winter months, when the body has less exposure to sunlight.

Experts across the world have been researching SAD since the beginning of the 1980s and have developed several theories about what may trigger the condition. We will consider them on the following pages.

Geographic Influences

Geographically, people who live in northern regions, where winters are longer and more persistent, are at higher risk for developing SAD. The percentage of those who are afflicted with SAD varies from region to region.

It is believed that as many as two to three percent of Canadians are affected by SAD, although current research is suggesting it may be as high as 5-10 %.

In the UK, there are statistics that indicate that 1 in 50 people are thought to have SAD or 2%. There are as many as 1 in 8 people that are not diagnosed in the UK that are thought just to experience the winter blues or 12.5% - a lesser form of the condition.

Overall Seasonal Affective Disorder is more common in countries that are further from the equator because countries near the equator experience more hours of sunshine throughout the year.

One U.S. study of SAD, found the rates of SAD were seven times higher among people in New Hampshire than in Florida which also suggests that the farther people live from the equator the most likely they are to develop SAD.

In the state of Alaska, as many as 8.9% of the population suffer from SAD while 24.9% suffer from the milder winter blues. Roughly 20% of Irish population is impacted by SAD with 10% of the population of the Netherlands now suffering from SAD.

Varying Degrees of SAD ☹

SAD appears in varying degrees. Therapies have indicated that some people who are impacted by SAD feel mildly depressed; while others are so depressed they require hospitalization. In others, their mood is unaffected, but their energy levels are so low that they are not likely to be able to accomplish the goals they would like to or would normally be able to achieve during o ther seasons.

So what can you do about SAD, short of taking a short vacation to Hawaii every few weeks during the winter? The remedies that follow that we have tested may provide the help that you need.

What are the Symptoms of SAD?

As mentioned before, the sufferers of the winter-onset type of SAD begin to develop their symptoms during the late fall or early winter, and then begin to taper off as spring approaches.

Symptoms usually appear rather mildly and become much more intense as the season progresses. Here is a list of some of the common symptoms of winter onset SAD:

1. **Depression** - In this case, it's persistent and continuous sadness or low "blue" mood. This symptom may be accompanied by weepiness, but not always.

2. **Lack of interest** - A severely significant loss of personal interests, or pleasure in activities, even for activities that are enjoyed regularly and often.

3. **Hopelessness** - In true hopelessness the sufferer believes is that no matter what he or she does, the situation will not improve and they will die from their personal depression and despair.

4. **Anxiety** - It is that sense of fear and anxiety, that state of painful uneasiness and apprehension, as to future uncertain situations.

5. **Loss of energy** - you are feeling nothing could get you up and moving, not even a holiday in the Hawaii that was a gift from your family or best friend. You're simply too tired to enjoy yourself.

6. **Heavy, "laden" feeling in the arms or legs** - It's almost as if someone put 5 kg. weights on your arms and 10 kg. weights on your legs ….

7. **Social withdrawal** - People who have Seasonal Affective Disorder, or winter-time blues, most likely do not want to have contact with others due to their feeling incommunicative.

8. **Oversleeping and other disturbed sleep patterns** - This might be realized in trouble in falling asleep or waking during the night and being unable to return to sleep.

9. **Noticeable loss of interest** in activities that you once enjoyed. This occurs over time. But, you see that loss occurring.

10. **Appetite changes, especially a craving for foods high in carbohydrates** - When this occurs, the next issue weight becomes apparent shortly thereafter.

11. **Weight gain** – Especially because of snacks in high carbs, increase of weight becomes the norm and weight control is difficult to achieve while experiencing SAD.

12. **Difficulty concentrating** – Because of the impact of apprehension, change in food intake, and the next few

areas of problems (following) the ability to focus one's thoughts is impaired.

13. **Agitation or slowing of movements** – The slowing of movements is far more common, by agitation may occur related to anxiety associated with the disorder.

14. **Poor concentration or indecisiveness.** For example, you may find it difficult to read, work, etc. Even simple tasks can seem difficult.

15. **Feelings of worthlessness, or excessive or inappropriate guilt** – When the symptoms mentioned are a part of daily life, feelings of worth are depleted, and shame of inability to be active or take action begins.

16. **In some extreme cases, Suicidal thoughts** in which a person may have recurring thoughts of death such as "life's not worth living" or "I do not care if I ever do not wake up again" are common. Sometimes these thoughts move into thoughts and even plans for suicide.

Having Ups & Downs, or is it SAD? 😦

Sometimes, it can hard to distinguish Wintertime SAD from the ups and downs we experience in the day-to-day lives that we all have. SAD is usually diagnosed if:

- ✓ You have at least five out of the above mentioned symptoms and
- ✓ Symptoms cause you to feel distressed or they compromise your normal functioning, such as affecting your work performance, and
- ✓ Symptoms occur most of the time on most days and have lasted at least two weeks, and
- ✓ The symptoms are neither due to a medication side-effect, nor due to drug or alcohol abuse, nor to a physical/ medical condition such as an underactive thyroid gland.

And remember symptoms do not always diagnose SAD. There are other symptoms to SAD, and there are other disorders to consider when looking at these symptoms. For instance, for those who have bipolar disorder, the spring and summer can bring on symptoms of mania or a less severe form of mania (hypomania), which is known as reverse SAD.

Summer Onset SAD and its Symptoms

The symptoms for summer onset SAD are included just so you can recognize the difference. This book only covers the winter onset SAD because there are far more people suffering from it and far more treatments available. These are some of the summer onset symptoms, but remember – they may apply to other disorders, including the more common winter variety.

- ✓ **Anxiety** – The summer version of SAD is more anxiety present than the winter one.
- ✓ **Trouble sleeping (insomnia)** – related to the anxiety and irritability part of the disorder.
- ✓ **Irritability** – The summer version of SAD tends to make people with the disorder hypersensitive to the amount of light they are exposed to causing …
- ✓ **Agitation** – Usually related to the above mentioned anxiety, insomnia and irritability.
- ✓ **Poor appetite** – Anxiety, irritability, agitation and insomnia all result in poor appetite which often results in:
- ✓ **Weight loss** – Weight loss is the common factor instead of weight gain.
- ✓ **Increased sex drive**

These symptoms tend to appear in the warmer and hot months of the year, and are less intense than the Winter-time version. We are hoping that sufficient research will present true diagnostic criteria for trials to discover a good treatment approach for the Summertime type of SAD, but as of yet, it's mostly unknown.

Starting the Day Off SAD 😮

Symptoms of SAD are often worse the first thing in the morning, every morning. It's normal to have some days when you feel down but if you feel down for days at a time and you cannot seem to get motivated to do activities you normally enjoy, consult your doctor.

This is especially crucial if you notice that your sleep patterns and appetite have changed or if you feel hopeless, think about suicide, or find yourself turning to alcohol or drugs for comfort or relaxation.

Along with these changes, be aware that people with SAD, like any other form of depression can often develop physical symptoms such as headaches, palpitations, chest pains, and general aches. This can complicate things, and it is not uncommon for a person to consult a doctor at first because they have physical symptoms such as chest pains. Patients, with chest pain symptoms, think they may have a problem like a heart condition, when it is actually due to SAD. It is increasingly common for SAD to cause physical symptoms.

Conquering Seasonal Affective Disorder In 7 steps

STEP 1:
Get Diagnosed

To help diagnose Seasonal Affective Disorder your doctor or mental health provider will do a thorough evaluation, which generally includes:

Detailed questions: Your physician will ask about your mood and seasonal changes in your thoughts and behavior. He or she may also ask questions about your sleeping and eating patterns, relationships, job, or other questions about your life. You might be asked to answer questions on a psychological questionnaire as well.

Your physician may do a physical examination to check for any underlying physical issues that could be linked to your depression.

Medical tests. There's no medical test for Seasonal Affective Disorder, but if your doctor suspects a physical condition may be causing or worsening your depression, you may need blood tests or other tests to rule out an underlying problem.

Technically...

Seasonal Affective Disorder is considered a subtype of depression (and/or bipolar disorder) in the diagnostics manual. Even with a thorough evaluation, it can be difficult for a physician to diagnose Seasonal Affective Disorder because other types of depression or other mental health conditions that might cause similar symptoms.

To be diagnosed with Seasonal Affective Disorder, you must meet criteria spelled out in the Diagnostic and Statistical Manual of Mental Disorders (DSM). *This manual is published by the American Psychiatric Association. It is used by mental health professionals to diagnose mental conditions and also by insurance companies to reimburse for approved treatments provided for such disorders.*

The following criteria must be met for a diagnosis of Seasonal Affective Disorder:

- ✓ You have experienced depression and other symptoms of SAD for at least two consecutive years, during the same season every year.
- ✓ The periods of depression have been followed by periods without depression.
- ✓ There are no other explanations for the changes in your mood or behavior.

If you have the symptoms of Seasonal Affective Disorder (SAD), visit your GP. If you are diagnosed with the condition, effective treatments are available. Your GP may carry out a psychological assessment to check your mental health. During the assessment, you may be asked questions about:

- ✓ your mood
- ✓ your lifestyle
- ✓ your eating patterns
- ✓ your sleeping patterns
- ✓ any seasonal changes in your thoughts and behavior
- ✓ whether there is anything in your personal history that may contribute to a depressive disorder, such as child abuse

✓ whether there is anything in your family history that may contribute to a depressive disorder, such as a family history of depression.

Your GP may also carry out a brief physical examination to check for any other possible causes of your symptoms.

SAD is often difficult to diagnose because there are many other types of depression that have similar symptoms. Therefore, it may take several years before you and your GP realize that your symptoms are forming a regular pattern.

Two major classification systems are used to diagnose depression. Your GP may use one of these systems to help diagnose SAD as opposed to chronic depression. The classification systems consider:

✓ the symptoms that you have
✓ how severe your symptoms are
✓ how long your symptoms last
✓ how your symptoms progress
✓ to what extent your symptoms prevent you from carrying out normal activities

Doctors usually diagnose Seasonal Affective Disorder based on the patient's description of symptoms, including the time of year the symptoms occur. There is also a diagnostic questionnaire called the Seasonal Pattern Assessment Questionnaire, or SPAQ, used in all Canadian University hospitals and widely used in the United States to assess SAD patients. And remember!

Don't Play Doctor with Yourself

It is very important that you do not diagnose yourself with Seasonal Affective Disorder. If you have symptoms of depression, see your doctor for a thorough assessment.

Sometimes, physical problems can cause depression. But other times, symptoms of seasonal depression are part of a more complex mental health issue problem.

A health professional should be the one to determine your level of depression and recommend the right form of treatment.

It can sometimes be hard to tell the difference between non-seasonal depression and SAD, because many of the symptoms are the same. To diagnose SAD, your doctor will want to know if:

- ✓ You have been depressed during the same season and have gotten better when the seasons changed for at least 2 years in a row.
- ✓ You have symptoms that often occur with SAD, such as being very hungry (especially craving carbohydrates), gaining weight, and sleeping more than usual.
- ✓ A close relative-a parent, brother, or sister - has had SAD.

STEP 2:
Acceptance

More often than not, the lack of acceptance drives the sufferer deeper into a downward spiral that doesn't end until the sun shines in.

Trying to be supportive of a friend or family member who is struggling with depression can be very challenging. This is often due to the denial that a sufferer goes through. No one wants to be labeled with a depressive disorder.

To the sufferer they then believe the world will shun them because they have this diagnosed mental disease needing treatment. The very nature of a psychological disorder of depression with a diagnosis code is enough to interfere with any individual's willingness or ability to seek out help and become a patient of a medical doctor, psychologist, psychiatrist and then follow through with treatment.

The denial stage begins when others suggest that you need a doctor because you are having symptoms that are unlike you. And, it gets worse if you do go to a doctor, psychologist or psychiatrist, who through their questioning you, determine that you have SAD and that you need anti-depressants, and other therapies for the long-hard winter. Almost all medical doctors and psychiatrists will say that. Don't worry, it's part of their required informed consent and medical protocol.

Most people simply deny this problem for a year, or more, until they or others realize that during the bright and light-filled summer months, they are a lot happier.

At that realization, they would know, if they got that realization during the summer – that they needed help during the winter months.

If the SAD sufferer got that realization during the high point of the Winter-time season, then it would be a good idea to implement the recommended therapies after a week or two at the beach in Hawaii, Mexico, etc. if at all possible, to accelerate getting the positive results possible.

There Are SAD Stories Too

I want to give you a not-so-typical SAD story. I want you to feel and listen into the emotion, and the result and consequences of non-treatment.

"Gigi and her husband Ivan (names changed, of course) lived in a city with nearly 4 million people, up at about 4,000 feet elevation, that got pretty grey and cold in winter. And, with her having undiagnosed SAD and her husband suffering in pain from the cold weather and multiple back and knee problems, they decided to move to the beach where they normally vacationed and were very happy in. Big Mistake!!! Big!

They vacationed in March-April, made arrangements to move in – for late July – and wouldn't you know it, they arrive, after a grueling long 11 hour drive on mountain roads with potholes, during a 3 day long rainstorm, to a house with no electricity, and a leaking roof.

Gigi starts crying … and even as the house improves, with electricity, later air conditioning, and lots of potential, just 2 blocks from the beach – Gigi cried every single day of the rainy season, but was better during the sunny days.

The next year, with some medication and counseling she was better during the rainy season until the hurricane hit – 'we're all gonna die tonight' and of course, no one died that night and there was no damage or risk to life, but she cried about it before it happened, during, and after it happened for a long time."

But that's only the beginning of the story. Trying to help someone in trouble, is just like someone putting a bulls eye on your forehead. For anything good and positive you put out in public and private, when faced with all the emotional craziness in front of you often transfers from one insane thought to the next. "You're to blame, YOU MADE US MOVE HERE." That was crazy rainy season talk.

It was bad, as the emotions of blaming became so difficult for him that her husband's visit to the doctor revealed horrible kidney problems in lab tests. To avoid feeling bad from her abusive words, when he was around her, he went out alone without Gigi only one – that one fateful day when he ate some street tacos, and within 24 hours was at home hemorrhaging all over the bathroom uncontrollably.

Wife screaming, they went to the doctor. Gigi nor the doctor believing the husbands story, and then he got an urge – ran to the bathroom, and bleed everywhere."

He was an intelligent man and realized he had allowed himself, an already crippled man with a weakened immune system, to be unintelligent regarding his eating due to emotions of being verbally abused by his wife who was raging during an episode of SAD.

He ran to eat some street food, tacos and soda, and VOILA – almost died trying to escape. Within 24 hours he was hemorrhaging and he was taken to a doctor, since there was no hospital for over 50 miles – URGHH, but he was treated immediately by the doctor, and bleeding stopped within a couple hours.

Then, later when his wife's diagnosis was discovered, by the way, it was SAD with anxiety disorder overlay, she refused to accept it – and only accepted medication for anxiety, get this ... if the prescription written to her husband's name, because nothing could be wrong with her. It must be HIM who was the one who had to have this disorder, even though she was in bed 20 hours a day crying and crying on Facebook to everyone, while he was working.

In Summary: Her husband is still with her, but not at a beach – but at a place in a valley where it is sunny every day of the year at least 12 hours. It helps with the SAD, but not the anxiety … he added.

STEP 3: Treatment and Getting a SAD light

Many options exist for treating SAD. They usually include treatment with light therapy, physical exercise, good nutrition, meditation, and yoga. The medical field will, most likely, recommend the use of antidepressant therapy for more pronounced and severe cases.

We will introduce to you a self-treatment plan that will help you combine many of these wonderful therapies and disciplines which will help you reduce and/or overcome the symptoms of Seasonal Affective Disorder.

From what has been researched, and what helps people with Seasonal Affective Disorder it would be fairly accurate to make the assumption the SAD develops from inadequate bright light, sunlight or the equivalent, during the winter months. Researchers have repeatedly demonstrated that bright light changes the chemicals in the brain. Exactly how this occurs and the details of its effects are yet exactly unknown, but they are currently being studied. Later on we will go over the mechanics of the brain and the disorder.

While the mechanisms of cause of the Seasonal Affective Disorder remain undetermined, the are some pretty clear factors that seem consistent like low vitamin D levels in the blood are found to be associated with a higher incidence of Seasonal Affective Disorder and some other depressive disorders.

Conventional treatment for Seasonal Affective Disorder may include Light therapy, medications and psychotherapy. If you have bipolar disorder, your doctor will be careful when prescribing light therapy or an antidepressant.

Caution: *Both treatments can potentially trigger manic episodes for those with bipilor disorder.*

With due respect for the allopathic medical field, we must take the time to talk about their use of conventional pharmaceutical medications for a part of the symptoms of Seasonal Affective Disorder. It is the duty of oneself and one's health care professional to make determinations regarding the use of brain-altering chemicals that could have a negative impact on the organs of your body. Will will neither recommend use of or recommend no use of.

Medical doctors, both general practitioners and psychiatrists, feel that some people with Seasonal Affective Disorder will experience temporary benefits from antidepressant treatment, especially if symptoms are severe. Antidepressants commonly used in the past to treat Seasonal Affective Disorder include fluoxetine (Prozac), sertraline (Zoloft), paroxetine (Paxil), and citalopram (Celexa) and venlafaxine (Effexor).

An extended-release version of the antidepressant bupropion (Wellbutrin XL) may help prevent depressive episodes in people with a longer history of Seasonal Affective Disorder.

Antidepressant medications, particularly those from the serotonin selective reuptake inhibitor family (SSRI) family, have been found to be effective temporary treatment for Seasonal Affective Disorder especially that form presents during the summer, but it also has some temporary benefit for Seasonal Affective Disorder which occurs during the fall or winter..

Since stimulant medications like modafinil (Provigil) may be a helpful addition to other treatments for Seasonal Affective

Disorder, other stimulants like methylphenidate (Ritalin) may play a future role in addressing this disease. We do not recommend either of these medications, nor do we not recommend them.

Acupuncture may be a viable alternative intervention to antidepressant medications, particularly in pregnant women, for whom medications should be used with particular caution. From personal experience from various acupuncture treatments from a rather older, experience acupuncture doctor, trained in China, I can honestly say that I see some improvement in physical and psychological health with acupuncture. For pregnant women, using it with Light Therapy, Meditation and Hypnotherapy is an en-light-ened alternative

Your doctor may recommend starting treatment with an anti-depressant medication weeks to a month before your symptoms typically begin each year. Also, your doctor might suggest that you continue to take an antidepressant medication beyond the time your symptoms normally go away. No comment.

Keep in mind that it may take several weeks to see full benefits from an antidepressant. In addition, you may have to try different medications before you find one that works well for you and has the least side effects.

Common side effects for this class of medications include insomnia, nausea, diarrhea and decreased sex drive or sexual performance.

Introduction to Light Therapy

Courtesy of: www.handyhealthcare.co.uk

Now, let's talk light therapy. First thing, remember that all lights are not created equal. This section will not only explain how to use light therapy, but how to buy the right for you.

In light therapy, also called phototherapy, you sit a few feet from a specialized light therapy box, lamp or bulb so that you're exposed to bright light. Light therapy mimics outdoor sun light and appears to cause a change in brain chemicals linked to mood.

Light therapy is one of the first line treatments for Seasonal Affective Disorder. It generally starts working in two to four days and causes few side effects. Research on light therapy is limited, but it appears to be beneficial for most people in relieving Seasonal Affective Disorder symptoms.

Before you purchase a light therapy box or consider light therapy, talk to your doctor or mental health provider to make sure it's a good idea and to make sure you're getting a high-quality light therapy box.

Daily, professionally supervised, phototherapy with exposure to a specific type of light, can often cause those struggling with Seasonal Affective Disorder to resolve symptoms more rapidly.

Phototherapy is a therapeutic level of a light that simulates the effects of the sun, which are delivered through a phototherapy device ("Light Box") that can be purchased or rented on a monthly basis from a private supplier, in medical device store, or bought online.

Many People –
Many Opinions

SAD Light Therapy products are extremely safe for most human beings, if you are generally healthy, you should have no problem adjusting to using one for treatment of SAD.

However, due to opinions presented here, we also urge you to consult a licensed healthcare provider before starting to use any lighting device. And, you should always consult one for the confirmed medical diagnosis of Seasonal Affective Disorder if you have insurance coverage. However, it's doubly important if you:

✓ Have vision problems or if you are sensitive to light.

✓ Are or recently have been taking antidepressants or medi-cation for treatment of epilepsy.

Online Suppliers

Due to the high risk nature of people's personal preference, opinions, or reactions, we will only display potential suppliers that we have discovered online. We hope that you will investigate a company thoroughly and their reputation with the Better Business Bureau, and the Attorney General's office before paying thousands of dollars for a device that might only actually require an investing of less than $500.

This medically approved unit is from Sphere Gadget Technologies and is only 59 dollars from Amazon. It is the required 10,000 lux, and it's a good unit for the price.

Sphere Gadget Technologies SP9882 Lightphoria Sad Light Therapy, 10,000 Lux

- ✓ Portable 10,000 lux energy light best for the winter times when you lack your daily dosage of sunlight.

- ✓ Emits a wide spectrum light wavelength creating a natural soothing glow - just like real sunlight!

- ✓ Selectable intensity levels - LOW (5,000lux), MEDIUM (8,000lux), HIGH (10,000lux) and programable 15, 30, 45 minute timer.

- ✓ Energy-efficient light lamp consumes only 7.2 watts and is rated for more than 20 years.

- ✓ Sleek lightweight design perfect for travel. 110v-240v world-wide voltage compatible. 1 year warranty provided by Sphere Gadget Technologies USA.

- ✓ http://www.amazon.com/gp/product/B004JF3G08/ref=as_li_qf_sp_asin_tl?ie=UTF8&camp=1789&creative=9325&creativeASIN=B004JF3G08&linkCode=as2&tag=lifeimprbook-20

A great starter light box at the right illumination for the job.

NatureBright SunTouch Plus Light and Negative Ion Therapy

This model seems to fulfill the minimum requirements for about $66.00.

The greatest list of suppliers of SAD Lights found on Amazon. co.uk includes medically certified SAD lights which are just as inexpensive as the ones that are not certified.

There is also:

- ✓ System includes 10,000-lux light therapy and negative ion therapy
- ✓ Balances your body clock, leaving you feeling rested, refreshed, and nourished all over
- ✓ http://www.amazon.com/gp/product/B000W8Y7FY/ref=as_li_tf_tl?ie=UTF8&camp=1789&creative=9325&creativeASIN=B000W8Y7FY&linkCode=as2&tag=lifeimprbook-20

But, Not the USA/FDA

Online Suppliers

But, as of today there is no medical certification for SAD Lights approved for the treatment of the condition of Seasonal Affective Disorder from the FDA, and in the US, there are no established standards and anyone can sell anything as a SAD therapy light box without controls or restrictions.

The reason for this is that the FDA and Medical Guidelines are yet to recognize the condition and most insurance companies will not pay for therapy under that diagnostic code. Be careful what you do, you have no protection from fraud, and you have no approved treatment of a REAL medical condition.

Realistically, maybe you should move to Europe or another area where the problem is recognized, treated, and the payment is by the government, not some insurance company who doesn't want to cover treatment because the FDA says – "let's see what pharmaceuticals come down the pike in the next decade for depression, before we approve a darn light bulb device for a medical condition and look like fools in front of the medical field."

And of course, there are still more options.

Caribbean Sun Box Light Therapy SAD Sunbox - Filters 100% of the UV rays

✓ Eases symptoms of Seasonal Affective Disorder (SAD) - Say goodbye to winter blues

✓ Latest technology uses powerful LED lighting emitting 10,000 LUX of light

✓ Proven results - doctor recommended - highly effective

✓ UV shielded Very low power consumption - only 9 watts - Filters 100% of the UV rays

✓ 10 year product warrantee

✓ http://www.amazon.com/gp/product/B0013LXYQW/ref=as_li_tf_tl?ie=UTF8&camp=1789&creative=9325&creativeASIN=B0013LXYQW&linkCode=as2&tag=lifeimprbook-20

SADelite 10,000 SAD Light Therapy Desk Lamp

✓ Unique, affordable, high quality product, compact and adjustable.

✓ Electronically powered - noflicker & no hum

✓ Uses only 80 watts - no heat

✓ Power : Universal - Lamp automatically selects from 110-270 volts, 50 or 60 hz.

✓ UV Output : blocked below 400 nm

✓ http://www.amazon.com/gp/product/B000NVW0YK/ref=as_li_tf_tl?ie=UTF8&camp=1789&creative=9325&creativeASIN=B000NVW0YK&linkCode=as2&tag=lifeimprbook-20

Uplift Technologies DL930 Day-Light 10,000 Lux SAD (Seasonal Affective Disorder) Lamp

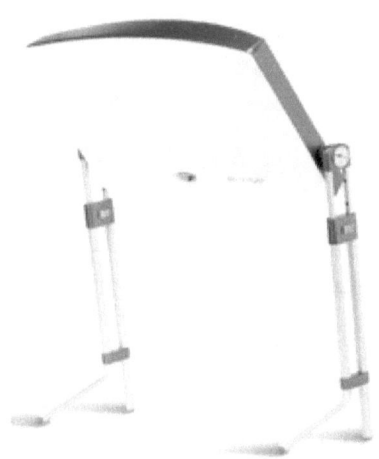

✓ Helps to ease seasonal mood swings and winter depression, and help improve sleeping patterns

✓ Features three fluorescent light tubes that combine to emit 10,000 lux of light

✓ Makes an exceptional task or reading lamp, and provides ambi-ent lighting

✓ UV filtered and safe, glare free, flicker free and has two light settings

✓ Can ease symptoms of SAD within one to two weeks of regular use

✓ http://www.amazon.com/gp/product/B0009MFUWC/ ref=as_li_tf_tl?ie=UTF8&camp=1789&creative=9325&creative ASIN=B0009MFUWC&linkCode=as2&tag=lifeimprbook-20

SunRay SAD Light Therapy Light Box 10,000 Lux

✓ The SunRay's moderate size, light weight and reasonable price have made it a very popular

✓ Used in Clinical Trials

✓ Two year guarantee on bulbs

✓ 10,000 lux at 18.5 inches

✓ 5,000 lux at 23 inches

✓ http://www.amazon.com/gp/product/B000KYYGD8/ref=as_li_tf_tl?ie=UTF8&camp=1789&creative=9325&creativeASIN=B000KYYGD8&linkCode=as2&tag=lifeimprbook-20

SunRay II SAD Light Therapy Light Box
Winter Blues

- ✓ Two light settings
- ✓ Detachable leg stands
- ✓ Ranges from 2500-10,000 lux
- ✓ Full set of bulbs included
- ✓ http://www.amazon.com/gp/product/B001KMAHY6/ref=as_li_tf_tl?ie=UTF8&camp=1789&creative=9325&creativeASIN=B001KMAHY6&linkCode=as2&tag=lifeimprbook-20

BlueMax 70 Watt Full Spectrum 10,000 Lux Light Therapy/SAD Desk Lamp

✓ Fully Dimmable from 100% to 20% using patented dimmable electronic ballast system.

✓ Scotopically enhanced, unique 5 phosphor blend allows you to see crisp clear colors as they are supposed to be seen.

✓ Can be used for both light therapy and as a high quality task lamp producing 10,000 lux at 18 inches and 5,000 lux at 28 inches.

✓ Powerful, energy-saving 70 watt lamp produces 4,300 lumens of brilliant full spectrum light equal to 300 watt halogen bulb.

✓ Lifetime warranty on the lamp 1 year on the bulb. Free shipping.

✓ http://www.amazon.com/gp/product/B008RXURTQ/ref=as _li_tf_tl?ie=UTF8&camp=1789&creative=9325&creativeASI N=B008RXURTQ&linkCode=as2&tag=lifeimprbook-20

Verilux HappyLite Deluxe Sunshine Simulator

- ✓ Get your daily dose of sunshine and boost your body's sense of well being
- ✓ Up to 10,000 LUX of Natural Spectrum Daylight alleviates symptoms associated with Winter Blues, jet lag, shift work and seasonal time changes
- ✓ Provides soothing, glare-free light
- ✓ Convenient, easy-to-use and portable
- ✓ http://www.amazon.com/gp/product/B0001ATEJ2/ref=as_li_tf_tl?ie=UTF8&camp=1789&creative=9325&creativeASIN=B0001ATEJ2&linkCode=as2&tag=lifeimprbook-20

Northern Light Technologies Nlt-fla Flamingo, Black

- ✓ 10,000 lux at 12 inches
- ✓ Made in North America
- ✓ UV blocked
- ✓ 7 years unlimited warranty
- ✓ Works on any household voltage around the world.
- ✓ http://www.amazon.com/gp/product/B003XDIPNA/ref=as_li_tf_tl?ie=UTF8&camp=1789&creative=9325&creativeASIN=B003XDIPNA&linkCode=as2&tag=lifeimprbook-20

Northern Light Technologies
Nlt-lux Luxor, White

- ✓ 10,000 lux at 11 inches
- ✓ Made in North America
- ✓ UV blocked
- ✓ 7 years unlimited warranty
- ✓ Modern looking
- ✓ http://www.amazon.com/gp/product/B0030MK31G/ ref=as_li_tf_tl?ie=UTF8&camp=1789&creative=9325&creati veASIN=B0030MK31G&linkCode=as2&tag=lifeimprbook-20

Sunrise SAD Therapy Light Box
w/ Dawn Simulator

✓ Bright up to 10,000 Lux LED light box

✓ Timer - when using the SRS 320 as a light box, the user can specify how long the light is on, from 10 - 90 minutes in 10 minute steps.

✓ Sunrise - the simulates a sunrise over a period of 0 (off), 15, 30, 45, 60, 75 or 90 minutes. Set to suit your preference.

✓ Sunset- simulates a sunset over a period of 15, 30, 45, 60, 75 or 90 minutes. Set to suit your preference.

- ✓ Full seven day alarm is provided to allow the user to set different times (if desired) on the alarm for different days of the week.

- ✓ The factory programmed time for all seven days is 07:00am.

- ✓ All functions of the Sunrise System 320 are indicated on the large backlit LCD display to clearly show the function being altered.

- ✓ A night light feature has also been included and the night light is user adjustable.

- ✓ A security feature that randomly turns the light full on and off between the times of 7:00pm and 9:00am can be set to operate when you are away from home.

- ✓ 12 or 24 hour clock display - you choose.

- ✓ http://www.amazon.com/gp/product/B0010AX7UY/ref=as_li_tf_tl?ie=UTF8&camp=1789&creative=9325&creativeASIN=B0010AX7UY&linkCode=as2&tag=lifeimprbook-20

Zadro Sunlight 365, Artificial Sunlight 365 Days a Year

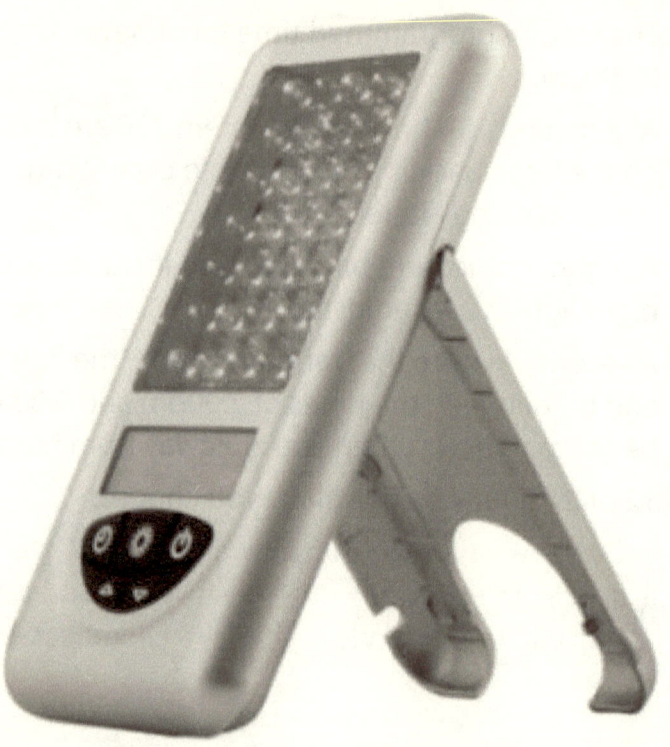

- ✓ 35pcs Blue LED's
- ✓ 10,000 LUX
- ✓ Light Intensity Adjustment
- ✓ Countdown Timer
- ✓ Desktop Clock
- ✓ http://www.amazon.com/gp/product/B002V2L6YO/ref=as_li_tf_tl?ie=UTF8&camp=1789&creative=9325&creativeASIN=B002V2L6YO&linkCode=as2&tag=lifeimprbook-20

Northern Light Technologies Nlt-box Boxelite, Black

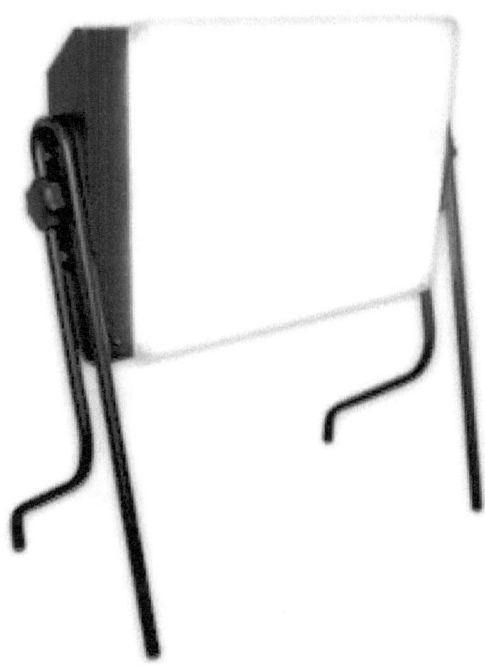

- ✓ 10,000 lux at 17 inches
- ✓ Made in North America
- ✓ UV blocked
- ✓ 7 years unlimited warranty
- ✓ Works on any household voltage around the world
- ✓ http://www.amazon.com/gp/product/B0011X554G/ref=as_li_tf_tl?ie=UTF8&camp=1789&creative=9325&creativeASIN=B0011X554G&linkCode=as2&tag=lifeimprbook-20

UK SAD Lights

For those living in the UK, here is a list of medically certified SAD Lamps.

SAD LIGHT THERAPY DAYLIGHT SUNLIGHT BOX LAMP 10,000 LUX

- ✓ Improve your energy-levels and combat Seasonal Affective Disorder (SAD), by Reicorp.
- ✓ The advanced curved shape focuses the light for maximum effect using 10,000 lux
- ✓ Complete with foldable tripod and wall mounting device
- ✓ Ideal for use in the home or office
- ✓ Compliant with the following certificates EN60601-1/-2, EC93/42, 2004/108/EC, EN60598, ISO13485, CE123
- ✓ http://www.amazon.co.uk/gp/product/B0011D3606/ref=as_li_qf_sp_asin_tl?ie=UTF8&camp=1634&creative=6738&creativeASIN=B0011D3606&linkCode=as2&tag=lifeimprbook-21

SAD Light Box - 10,000 lux - Medically Certified - Seasonal Affective Disorder - Light Therapy Lamp - Updated and Improved Winter 2012/2013 Model

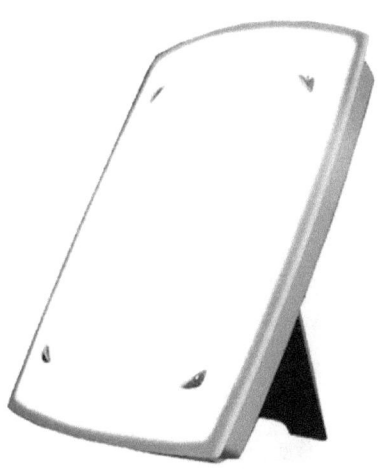

- ✓ This item is VAT Free! Please see main description for terms & conditions, by Redstone Technologies
- ✓ Updated Winter 2012-2013 Model
- ✓ 2 x 36W Energy Saving Light Tubes (approx 8000 hours of usage)
- ✓ *12 month gurantee* + Medically Certified
- ✓ Size: 30 x 10 x 48cm. Mains Adapter. Reflective Cover, Folding Tripod
- ✓ http://www.amazon.co.uk/gp/product/B000YSDHZ8/ ref=as_li_qf_sp_asin_tl?ie=UTF8&camp=1634&creative=67 38&creativeASIN=B000YSDHZ8&linkCode=as2&tag=lifeimp rbook-21

Medically Phototherapy Unit SAD Light Box Therapy Lamp DAVITA Vitabright 70

✓ Medical product certified according to EU directive 93/42/EWG

✓ High quality plastic housing

✓ Housing measures: H= 46 cm; W= 30 cm; D= 7 cm

✓ Connected load: 72 watts

✓ max. lighting power: 15.000 Lux

✓ http://www.amazon.co.uk/gp/product/B009HE8822/ ref=as_li_tf_tl?ie=UTF8&camp=1634&creative=6738& creativeASIN=B009HE8822&linkCode=as2&tag= lifeimprbook-21

Lumie Arabica SAD Lightbox

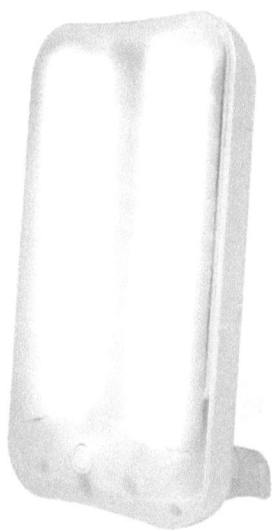

- ✓ Lumie lightbox to lift your mood, boost concentration and restore your natural energy
- ✓ Can treat the symptoms of SAD (seasonal affective disorder) and winter blues
- ✓ Simply switch it on and position it close by while you're on the PC or watching TV
- ✓ Recommended treatment time is 60 minutes at 50 cm
- ✓ Lumie Arabica is certified as a medical device, so you can be sure you're getting a product that's been specifically designed for light therapy use
- ✓ http://www.amazon.co.uk/gp/product/B0031IITEC/ref=as_li_tf_tl?ie=UTF8&camp=1634&creative=6738&creativeASIN=B0031IITEC&linkCode=as2&tag=lifeimprbook-21

Full Spectrum Lighting Lite Pod/SAD Light - Medically Certified

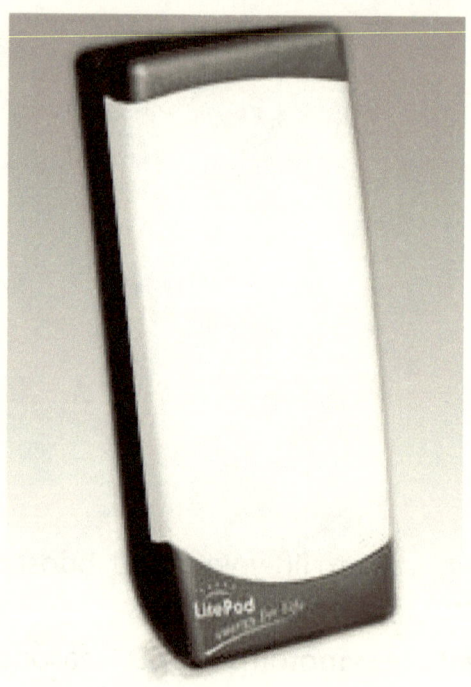

- ✓ Size 38 x 12.5 x 12.5 cm
- ✓ Small, discrete and stylish
- ✓ Treatment time 45 minutes to 1 hour
- ✓ Class 11A medical device
- ✓ Perfect for use in the office or around the home
- ✓ http://www.amazon.co.uk/gp/product/B00117X37I/ref=as_li_tf_tl?ie=UTF8&camp=1634&creative=6738&creativeASIN=B00117X37I&linkCode=as2&tag=lifeimprbook-21

Aurora - SAD Lamp - Medically Certified - Designer Lamp

✓ Weight: 2.2KG

✓ Dimensions: 63 cm Height and diameter 20cm

✓ Light Source: 2 x 36W

✓ Luminosity: 10000 Lux

✓ Therapy Distance: 23cm - 75 min

✓ http://www.amazon.co.uk/gp/product/B004J8078E/ref=as_li_tf_tl?ie=UTF8&camp=1634&creative=6738&creativeASIN=B004J8078E&linkCode=as2&tag=lifeimprbook-21

SAD LIGHT THERAPY LIGHT 10,000 LUX DAYLIGHT LAMP

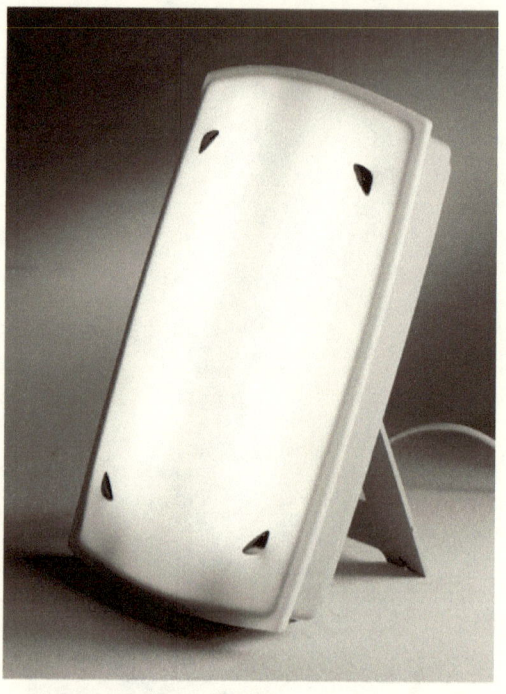

✓ This daylight lamp uses very bright light (10,000 lux) to simulate natural sunlight.

✓ CE Certified

✓ Medically proven this is a certified medical device.

✓ http://www.amazon.co.uk/gp/product/B002Y0FU0Y/ref=as_li_tf_tl?ie=UTF8&camp=1634&creative=6738&creativeASIN=B002Y0FU0Y&linkCode=as2&tag=lifeimprbook-21

SAD Light Summary

So, what we have given you is information on the basic, Light Box for treatment of Seasonal Affective Disorder. The British version is approved as medically effective.

The US doesn't have the FDA regulatory control of Light Boxes as of yet. The units may include add-ons like a negative ion generator which supposedly generates better moods and perhaps some have Aromatherapy atomizers built in. Whatever rocks your boat! This is not medically certified, and it is buyer beware, so be aware!

Honestly speaking, if it works for you and I truly believe it will - who am I to criticize. Some people have questions about these 10,000 lux lights, and they include: Will using the Light box give me a suntan? And regretfully, I must tell you no – there is no suntan in a box available for you in this program.

Another question relates to: Is there a risk of UV overexposure with the Light Box. And again, there is no risk of UV any more than any other light bulb.

Before you spend money on a better, or more purposeful Light Box, you need to get one that will give you the correct therapy for the environment that you are going to be using it.

When searching for a product that you are going to be using from one season to the next and season after season – for 10 years or more … you need to take into consideration … length of time for treatment, cost of the unit, and how portable it is. Also, take guarantee and service into consideration:

Questions To Ask Yourself Before You Buy A Long Term Use SAD Light:

- ✓ How long must I spend with each light box therapy treatment? (it usually varies from 20 - 90 minutes each treatment.)
- ✓ Will I take a treatment at home and work and need something light weight and portable?
- ✓ Where should I position my light box and therefore, at what distance should the light box be placed from my eyes? (Different light therapy devices are effective at different distances)
- ✓ How much can I afford to pay? (Certified medically proven Light boxes vary in price).

Questions To Ask Companies
Selling SAD Light Boxes:

✓ Describe your condition; ask them which product they recommend for your situation and why.

✓ Is this product proven effective for the treatment of SAD?

✓ How much does it cost?

✓ How much for delivery?

✓ Cost of replacement parts?

✓ Dimensions and weight, portability?

✓ What is the recommended treatment time?

✓ Does it have a two year warranty? Is an extended warranty available?

✓ Returns policy in case it doesn't work for me?

Insurance Coverage

As of March 1, 2013 the FDA (Federal Drug Agency) had not issued any approval for SAD lights and therefore, Blue Cross/Blue Shield does not cover the costs of Light therapy.

In the scope of what's covered or not covered, we defer to the insurance companies and in the United States the Federal Drug Administration which makes the decisions of whether something is *medically-certified* and at this point, there are no light box devices approved for the treatment of Seasonal Affective Disorder by the FDA.

You will find lies online, but when you search for medically approved or medically certified SAD lighting on Amazon.com who tends to love making profits … you know that nothing is available; otherwise they'd be selling it.

LED SAD Lights vs. Traditional SAD Lights

In the most recent research, LED light boxes are becoming more popular for SAD treatment and seem to be as effective for treating Seasonal Affective Disorder as traditional tube bulb SAD Light devices.

The British Season Affective Disorder support organization www.SAD.org.uk now recommends LED Light-boxes along with conventional tube bulb light therapy devices.

For many years, Philips Lighting, previously Norelco (and North American Philips), – became aware of the impact of improved lighting on office productivity. Over the years, they developed a line of lights that were very advanced for improving life.

Right now I want to introduce you to one of their most modern devices which is an LED light therapy devices that actually has met with great success in the treatment of Seasonal Affective Disorder.

http://www.amazon.co.uk/gp/product/B002G1Y8S6/ref=as_li_qf_sp_asin_il_tl?ie=UTF8&camp=1634&creative=6738&creativeASIN=B002G1Y8S6&linkCode=as2&tag=lifeimprbook-21

NEWEST TECHNOLOGY AVAILABLE

Philips HF3330 goLITE BLU Energy SAD Light

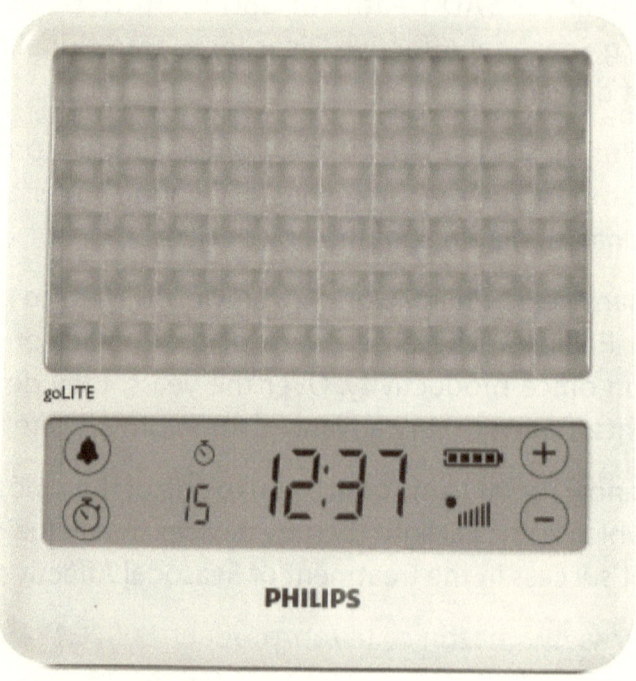

Philips HF3330 goLITE BLU provides the specific spectrum of light our bodies respond to. Advanced diffusion optics and less intense than 10,000 lux white light provide a soft, even light with a wider treatment field for flexibility. Philips HF3330 goLITE BLU is fully programmable and allows you to save your personal settings. The backlit touch screen provides easy programming and the built-in clock and treatment alarm reminds you when to use it.

Full-Spectrum White Light Treatment

Philips was the great push in the development and sales of the Full-Spectrum White Light. Although there is some controversy as to which is the most effective treatment for SAD, it has repeated shown to be beneficial to those struggling with SAD.

There seems to be various treatments with Full-Spectrum White Light as it is not 10,000 Lux strength and very often both humans and plants respond positively to exposure to Full-Spectrum lighting all day, all night.

Using Full-Spectrum White Light as active treatment for SAD, people can read, but not sleep, for a few hours a day and during the light therapy they can also do other things as well, depending on the configuration of the Light Therapy equipment. You can equip a whole room or home with Full-Spectrum lighting by using fluorescent ceiling fixtures to light up the entire room.

Symptoms should begin to subside within the first week of your beginning with Full-Spectrum as your choice of your first Light Therapy. And, you also know that Light Therapy is a treatment of a symptom. When the use of the Light Therapy stops, the symptoms tend to reappear.

Full-Spectrum Lighting has proven effective in the prevention of future episodes of Seasonal Affective Disorder, regular exposure to lights that are bright, particularly special fluorescent lights, significantly improves depression in people suffering from SAD when it presents during the fall and winter.

Full-Spectrum lighting is available at lighting stores everywhere.

STEP 4: Developing a Routine

Dawn Meditation

This is the most simple of meditations, as you begin about 20 minutes before the sun rises, and you will position yourself as you see below.

Of course, if you are inside, it's more likely to look like this:

And if you want you can add candles behind you in the room, crystals, or gemstones, or anything you believe in that will help you to meditate peacefully.

You enter the position, notice that you are facing the sunrise through an open window or directly facing the sunrise itself while you meditate outdoors.

Your point of focus is the opening light that is soon to be born. And as you look in that direction, you know with all your intelligence and feeling that … when you complete the meditation you will have Light in your life, greater than before.

Focus on your breathing.

Focus your attention and awareness on your breathing. Make your breath very slow, very deep and very relaxed. Your breathing is intrinsically connected to your thoughts and your emotions so by calming your breath you inherently calm your thoughts and emotions.

Imagine yourself on the shore of a deserted Hawaiian island at just before dawn and the sun is beginning to appear just over the horizon. Hear the gentle rise and fall of the waves as they wash up onto the sand. Feel the warmth of the first rays of sun caressing your face. See the beautiful colors dancing on the wispy clouds.

Now, move your hands into the mudra position – pictured below:

The mudra position of the hands above intensifies the effect of relaxation and inner peace, something you really, really want.

With each inward breath you notice the waves gently wash up onto the shore and with each outward breath the waves gently recede. Your breath is controlling the movement of the waves. The slower you breathe the slower the movement of the waves.

After a while you slowly rise and wade into the cool, clear, refreshing water. As you wade in deeper and you find this ocean is washing away any remnants of fear, doubt, disbelief, and all of the worries that may have been clinging on in your mind. This water is cleansing you to the very depth of your soul.

You find yourself miraculously dissolving into the ocean until you no longer exist as an individual – you have become the ocean.

Now with each breath you find your awareness, your consciousness expanding. Your essence is now stretching from horizon to horizon, from infinity to eternity. And still your find yourself expanding with each inward breath. Become absorbed in this inner expansion, this inner awakening.

Gradually, while still maintaining this remarkable sense of expansion you find yourself becoming the sun, naturally, and glowing, and lighting up your whole universe and then you return to your normal existence but with a new enriched with light and a rewarding sense of expanded self and your own inner light.

The sun is starting to awaken by now, it is time, and when you start this meditation at the right time – the sun awakens by the time you have reached this point. *(If there in no sun, then the SAD Light box should be programmed to come on at this point in the meditation, or a few moments before).*

Now, if you wish, you might chant, or sing. And when you feel the sunlight, or you feel the light of the light box on you (make sure that the light box is now on), you might feel like … chanting …Aum… Aum… Aum …. Aum, and sing *"Sunlight on my shoulder makes me happy, sunlight on my eye can make me cry, sunlight on the water, looks so lovely, sunlight almost always makes me high."*

Make sure your meditation lasts for as long as needed so that you can have another 20 minutes of focus on the light source. If you live in a northern area, you need to be equipped with the proper light box to use in addition to meditation.

That was a sample Dawn meditation – meditation at sunrise to open your mind and heart to allow Light to come into your life. Please practice and continue with the following very simple evening meditation before sleep.

Along with this, you need a healthy breakfast to start your day. You should also consider a yoga routine (amplified by your SAD light of course) as well as incorporating healthier habits into your work, like a healthy lunch/ evening meal depending on your shift and, hypnosis to sleep or more meditation with your sadlight.

STEP 5:
Learning to Meditate

For many years, meditation has been used in the east by anyone from supposed holy men to the common people. Today, in the west and around the world, medical studies have recently put this practice to the test, applying as a treatment for stress, depression and anxiety.

A news story India reports that a Washington State Landscape artist, Jane Anderson, like most people had been struggling with SAD during the cold months for a long, long time. After discovering and applying the meditation, she noticed positive changes occurring within 30 days.

Intrigued, Anderson then researching the topic as an undergraduate student, together with a team of University students, wanted to know if there was a change in brain activity after such a short time.

At the beginning of the new study, each participant would have an EEG, a measurement of the brain's activity that could be monitored in real time, according to a Wisconsin university statement.

Then, one group was invited to take part in meditation training while the other group was told they would be trained later.

The group was then offered two ½ hour sessions per week, and encouraged to practice as much as possible between sessions. But, they were not given any set measure for how much they should practice.

People who had done the meditation showed a greater proportion of activity in the left frontal region of the brain, in response to subsequent attempts to meditate as compared to the group which did not meditate.

Here's Why That's So … Important!

The frontal lobes of the brain are the most anterior, which means they are positioned right behind your forehead and at the top-front of your head. There is a left lobe and a right lobe.

The frontal lobe is surrounded by five other very important brain sections: the parietal lobe, the occipital lobe, the cerebellum, the brainstem, and the temporal lobe.

These are integral to our humanity, and how we live, act and think as this is in basically our control system. The "essence" of our humanity, according to Dr. Donald Stuss of The Rotman Research Institute.

The cerebral cortex (our aforementioned "control system," or the "frontal lobes") is the seat of our emotions and judgments related to sympathy. Sympathy is the ability to feel sorrow for someone else's suffering, and empathy, which has the capability to understand people's feelings and problems.

This is what makes us human. They are also the seat of understanding humor, including subtle witticisms and idioms of wordplay, recognizes sarcasm and irony.

They are also where recognition of deception occurs. The frontal lobes control the processes called "mentalizing" upon which our socialization is based; this is the ability to understand another's mental processes.

These all-important lobes are not identical in function; there is significant asymmetry between the left and right lobes. The left is predominantly language related while the right is mostly non-verbal.

You've probably heard that the left brain is the logical, which tends to be language based, and the right is creative, which tends to be non-verbal.

In fact, you may know or be an artist who cannot respond verbally while immersed in the creative -- right brain, non-verbal -- process.

It is significant to note, however that modern technological advances in MRIs, PETs and CT Scans show that many people pose exceptions to this left/right divide because their brains involve both lobes in nearly all behaviors.

In fact, one suggestion is that hook-handed writers, those who arc their wrists and write toward themselves have full language dominance on left and right, with no subordination at all between the lobes.

The frontal lobes are of paramount significance in determining our daily capabilities, personality manifestations, social interactions and judgments and decisions.

The cerebral cortex or frontal lobes are indeed the seat of our essence and nature. Meditation, as evaluated by thousands of years of history, and recently evaluated by the AMA has been judged effective for treatment of stresses.

The less stress a person holds inside of themselves, the less depression the will feel under any circumstances. Meditation is proven effective for all forms of depressive disorders.

If you meditate for 20-30 minutes a day in front of your light box your frontal lobes will soon light up like a Christmas Tree making you a far happier person.

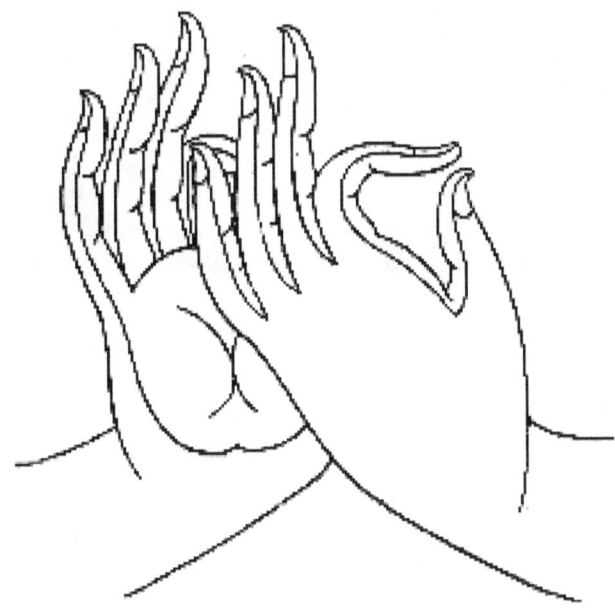

Meditation Study

Give yourself about 20 to 30 minutes a day to work with meditation. However, if your goal is less than 20 minutes, you must remember that any form of stress control meditation usually requires at least 20 minutes daily. Either way you will find yourself in a completely different, better frame of mind.

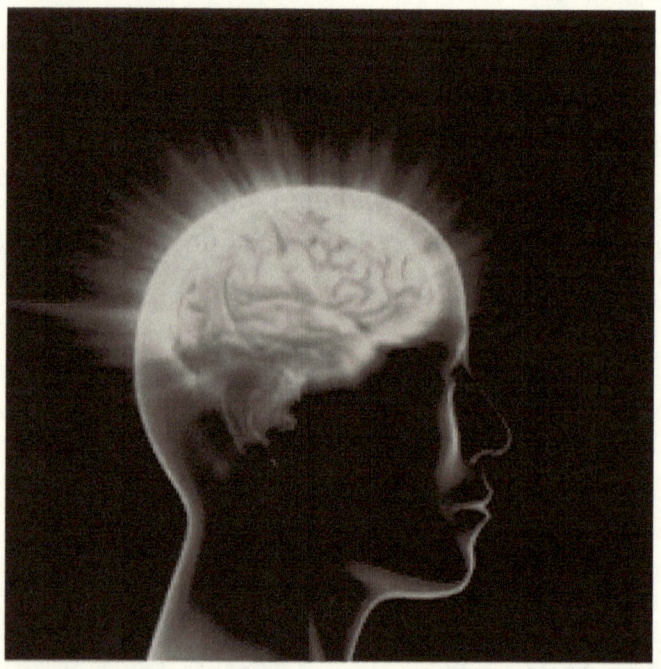

As a beginner, don't let the process of meditation worry you. The fact is that it's easy to understand if you are willing to invest the time and go from normal mind to the focal concentration of meditation. It is certainly worth every effort to get there.

Our process of meditation is a very simple and basic process that is aimed at helping you to reach the next stage of mind development, and that includes a semi-self-hypnosis method for SAD. So let's start first with the first step, meditation, for now, and we'll help you graduate into a method that will help you remove most of the symptoms of sad, and make you far more happy.

Stage One: The Normal Mind

In the "normal mind" state, your mind is working in many directions simultaneously. Under the normal functions, it bounces back and forth, from one thought to another, from one worry to another and so on.

And, when you do get a positive thought in there somewhere – it's quickly shuffled off to oblivion (that's located somewhere deep in your subconscious mind, with other thoughts) in the 4:1 ratio of negative to positive. You focus more on things happening, in reality, that don't make you feel so good.

If you consider how the mind is supposed to work for success … this normal mind behavior is not normal at all.

We need to focus less on negatives if we want to accomplish more positive things and succeed at the solving of all our life problems.

Stimulus from everywhere comes into your mind simultaneously. If you doubt that, look at CNN World News. You have on CNN one news story on visual, with run screen text summary about it, and below that's a running banner of current news events, and then the urgent notices of world calamities. Yes, your mind gets bombarded on CNN and everywhere else as well.

When something new stimulates your mind, you remember it,, and you move on to a new thought. You do that with every thought that comes to mind. Scientists guesstimated the average normal thinking person in the US has 60,000 thoughts per day, most of those thoughts they are totally unaware of.

If you saw this happening in a graphic you would see a head bombarded with thoughts, 20% positive, 80% negative, simultaneously, sorting them out and filing them for future use.

Some with tags would indicate UNIMPORTANT - NEVER ACTIVATE. Others would be tagged saying VITAL DATA or EMOTIONAL REACTIONS and several other tags exist also.

You can see the effect of 60,000 thoughts daily, and the effect of dreams with messages. And, although you might feel like that cartoon is depicting you completely out of control during this gremlin attack – you probably are totally in control and a totally responsible person.

No Control Over Bombarding Thoughts

You have very little control over the way you behave and think while this thought bombardment occurs. Behavior at that point often becomes automatic. Not only does your mind go from one thought to another rather quickly, but as you might imagine, your physical body is doing the same thing.

Everything is on autopilot. Various systems in your body are impacted by the subject or quality of your specific thoughts. So are your emotions and feelings.

Let me give you one example: Let's say that you are in a car driving home. In your mind, you see your newborn son, and this you see while you are driving. Your mind goes thinking simultaneously from control of the car to your child. You see him as precious, snuggled between you and your wife, at home when you are lying in bed watching TV. *Positive imagery.*

He's the love of your life. Then, your mind moves to thoughts from your own childhood. You feel happy and smile at the feelings and memories. Your whole body and mind feels better.

But, sometimes, these memories don't always play out so nicely. You can go through the same emotional processes and recall negative images and memories, too. Things you had tagged and stored deeply in your subconscious under UNIMPORTANT - NEVER ACTIVATE still can impact you.

Let's look at another example. Consider that the child you saw was not your own and he's a teenager doing something that he shouldn't be doing, maybe like hanging with the wrong bunch, jacking a car, and getting drunk or getting high. *Negative imagery.*

Now, you are wondering about your own children, what they are doing, that you don't even know about. Your emotions will then follow you too with thoughts that are fearful and tense.

Here is how you can become easily distracted by thoughts running through your mind which then directly impacts the way you drive your vehicle and whether or not you will get home to be with your own child. The emotion is negative, and the label we give it is FEAR.

The lesson that every person on earth must learn is that:

FEAR means …

 **F**alse
Evidence
Appearing
Real

People get afraid from FEAR and make big mistakes, and perhaps while thinking about your child, you'd run a red light or narrowly miss having a accident.

As you can see, while you are in your normal state of mind, your emotions as well as your physical body are at risk. Each plays their role in the outcome of these events.

Most frequently stress builds up during this mental process, and since it is our "normal mind" state, this stressful condition just piles up over time. Soon, you might find yourself unable to focus on anything. With your thoughts working overtime, you might even have trouble balancing activities in your everyday life.

In summary … your "normal" way of thinking could be considered as one of the worst ways that you can live your life. But, do you have a choice?

Stage Two: Focal Concentration

When you enter into a state of concentration, you first enter a state of intense focus which will lead you to meditation. Don't confuse concentration with meditation. It's different, and concentration is only a small process leading to meditation. During the second stage of meditation, you will start to gain control of your mind.

Once you learned to achieve this type of mind condition, chances are good that you can improve the quality of your life considerably.

In this focal concentration mind stage, your goal appears to be simple, but in reality, it's quite difficult to master to any significant degree. You must concentrate/focus on one sole thing or one object for extended periods of time. In the old days of meditation, it was contemplation on your navel. Today, it's totally your choice!

To be successful, you must keep your mind focused absolutely and only on that 'one thing' and not permit yourself to be distracted by anything. Just focus on it, without permitting your mind to wander. Actually, this is one of the most difficult parts of the training – focus without wandering.

During concentration mind stage, you'll discover that although the process of focusing on one element seems simple enough, the problem is the mind's tendency to try to trick you back into its "normal" mind state of being. By consistent practice and discipline you will be able to prevent the mind from being pulled back.

For example: let's say that you a need to develop focal concentration, on a research paper ... a report. You sit down think, and begin working. You are allowing your mind to focus and simultaneously relax while concentrating on the topic at hand.

You think about the topic and you can even clearly visualize what the topic is about. Then, all of a sudden, in the midst of concentrating on the report, you start to think of what you co-worker said about your paper. That distracting and unrelated thought leads back to thoughts of what that co-worker said something about your secretary's provocative blouse. Within minutes, you are no longer thinking about this important report – but instead, you're starting to unbutton her blouse. *Normal Mind!*

The bottom line is that the distraction reverted your thinking to the "normal mind" stage, and you've accomplished little in the way of concentration. That's not going to help you achieve your purpose.

Your goal on concentration is to be aware of what is happening. When you realize that you've been distracted and recognize that your mind has fooled you into making its own decisions all you need to do is refocus and concentrate.

When you master the art of keeping your mind focused and concentrated, you will experience a new type of thinking -- clarity.

For a person who has SAD to be that relaxed and to be able to feel better about your life, that's an amazing feeling.

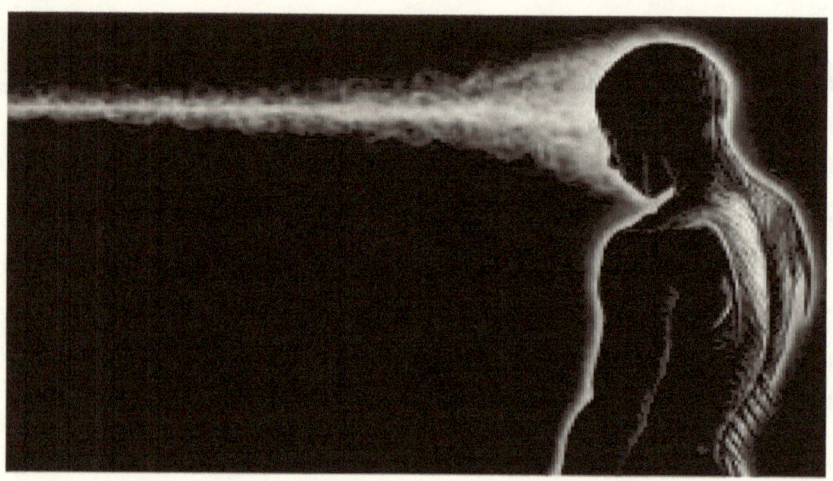

Your Focused Mind Is The Most Powerful Force On This Planet.

Stage Three: Final Meditation

The third state in meditation is when you enter a totally different realm. At this point, you are able to totally concentrate on an object or thought without falling for any type of distraction. Here, no distractions or mind tricks occur during the meditation.

This is the stage to strive for because it really can offer you a new way of seeing things. You will be able to focus more clearly and in the process you'll understand and learn more. You will make better decisions that are focused.

During the concentration segment, your mind only concentrates on the objects you present to it in a minimal way.

Distraction tends to break the continuous stream of concentrated thoughts, leaving you with having to recognize the problem and to go back and fix it.

Meditation is Different

In meditation, you are keeping an ongoing stream of thought moving. There's nothing breaking it and nothing that is able to pull your mind from it. This is the ultimate experience in meditation because of the amount of focus it provides you. As an example of what meditation can do for you, consider this, If you think about just one topic, over and over again, anything and everything connected to that topic will probably manifest in your life -- in one form or another. Let's say that the word you use is 'love'.

If you think of love in meditation, you concentrate on that one word which leads to other love terms. You love something; you love someone, different types of love, and so on.

Eventually, you are connected virtually every way possible to love. You physically feel it, you emotionally feel it. You think everything about it. And, eventually, you have connected everything to love.

When you achieved this type of meditation, you will have elevated yourself to a new enlightenment. You've gone far beyond the level of concentration and you now enter the final stages of meditation called contemplation.

This part of the final stage of meditation is the very best level of consciousness that your mind and body can enter. Although it takes some time to work through these various processes to achieve this level, the end result is well worth it.

Stage Four: Contemplation

Contemplation is the final stage of meditation. In this mind state, virtually anything and everything is possible.

Not many people experience this level nor understand it. During the stage of contemplation, you enter an entirely new world of thought and mind. It is a different dimension beyond yourself and your own problems – it is your interconnection with the entire Universe and the Source (God). At this level, your body and mind are released. Now, you are experiencing a level of inner consciousness that permits you to connect with silent thought, to the entire Universe and the Source.

When this occurs, you will realize that you are part of a much grander scheme of things. You know that you are just one small part of a very large world, a microcosm of the macrocosm.

The key to contemplation is the ability to become united with the totality of all this.

When you obtain this highest level of meditation, you enter into the state of realization of Cosmic Consciousness and Oneness. You actually, now, have entered into an enlightened, meaningful and connected level.

Those who practice meditation know that this stage of being. Being ONE with the highest form of meditation is what you should be attaining. Most long term meditators feel that it is something that you are born with -- the yearning for and talent to achieve this level.

Think about how your mind works today, right this second. How does it feel? Are you thinking about this process while you are reading it, or is your mind playing jingles from your favorite commercial, or Christmas music, if it is seasonably appropriate.

Or, as you are reading, are your kids screaming for your attention? Remember, that each time you face any distraction your mind is pulled to another direction making it nearly impossible for you to focus and to obtain true meditation.

However, true detachment is something that you can learn. In fact, it is something that you are born with, that is, the ability to achieve as your birthright.

We are going to begin with simple meditations that you can do, or record, and playback to yourself. Read them first to understand instructions, then record them or have someone with a gentle and wonderful voice record them for you.

Then play the recording to yourself and follow the instructions.

STEP 6:
Hypnosis session from SAD to HAPPY

Hypnosis with Light Therapy

Hypnosis therapy is similar to meditation, in that you can do it with your Light box, or in sunlight with your eyes closed, and that you can do with Dawn Simulation Machine and/or with SAD Light Therapy Boxes, and that you can it use when you awaken or when you go to sleep at night, or anytime you feel you need a short vacation to Hawaii.

We are providing scripts for you for experiencing a dawn awakening hypnosis, one for going to sleep, and another for a visit to a private beach in Hawaii. Also, you can write to info@lifeimprovementbooks. com and ask for the free audios for these hypnotherapy scripts, so you just have to listen to the voice of Dr. Jay Polmar, and you will go deep asleep and gain the benefits while in the hypnotic state.

Procedure for Listening to Hypnosis with light Therapy

Allow about twenty minutes twice a day.

Hypnosis & Visualization with Light Source. (record for playback)

Get comfortable either sitting up in a chair nearly your Light box, with your back straight and your feel flat on the floor or sitting in a cross legged (semi-lotus) position, and close your eyes.

Now is the time to completely relax... make a conscious effort to relax your body as completely relaxed as possible, each time I mention the word relax.

For the next few minutes, just focus on your breathing. To the best of your ability, feel your lungs... feel how they feel. consciously know how they feel while they're completely expanded and filled with air, pure clean air that you are inhaling, healing purifying oxygen going into your lungs and oxygenating your blood carrying healing energy to every part of your body. And, now see how they feel after you exhaled your breath and all the carbon dioxide has left your body. You feel calm and pure. Calm, cleansed by pure air and pure thought.

Just know that when performing the healing meditation, there's no right or wrong way of doing this -- you are already doing this now. So, draw in another deep, deep breath and feel the lungs filled.

Whatever you feel at this level is just perfect for you. All you're doing now is relax, that's fine, just relaxing is great because it's reducing stress and tension, and you are finding that you have nothing to worry about. Worries come to mind, and you no longer react to them.

Just like a balloon ... worries float away into the higher atmosphere and pop, and ... GONE. As you will see, worries just begin to disappear because you no longer think about them or react. You are calm, clear and detached, no matter what you think. It's okay you'll get through it with a clear mind and without emotional reaction. Clear mind, with no emotional reaction, you have only a clear mind.

If a worrisome thought or any thought comes to take your focus away, just take a deep breath, listen and understand the meaning of my words as you let the unimportant worrisome thought just float away.

You now realize that this is not the time for you to be worrying about any of the things that might, could, should would, happen in your day-to-day life, nor is it time to think about 'what if this should happen or that should happen'. Forget the mights, the coulds, the

 *shoulds, the woulds, and what if's right now …. They do not serve any good purpose in your life whatsoever.*

This is your time, to just let go, let your head down, and for a very short period of time, you can completely relax every part of your body. You know that you are never out of control. You feel completely secure in this meditative hypnosis relaxation.

Now, again, focus on your lungs. See them in your mind's eye. See if you can see them filled with pure clean air. See them when they are empty. See how relaxed you are feeling. And if your mind drifts away from your lungs, just bring your focus slowly back to where you need to be focused - on your breathing.

You are doing nothing wrong and everything that you do will be a success. And, if you hear my voice, that's great! And if you are d-e-e-p that you don't hear my voice, that's fine, too. You can be sure that your subconscious is receiving the message with every word that I say. You hear and understand every word I say.

Now, in your mind's eye-- just in the center of your forehead - in the center of your brow, you can see some words all lit in retro neon... and the words say

RELAX – LIGHTEN UP

Now see the words RELAX – LIGHTEN UP now being about a foot in front of your forehead... see them now about a foot in front of your forehead, the words RELAX – LIGHTEN UP. And now inside your mind's eye, see the words, and you just relax and lighten up.

Now this is a process, just like when you were young and you didn't yet know how to ride a bicycle, or didn't know how tell time on a clock, or even read the simplest book.

And later on, when you had learned to ride your bike, tell time, and read you were so excited about being able to do each of these things and while you were having such a great time, you lost track of time because you were so INTO what you were doing and were so excited about being able to do it. That's how you learned.

Learning to RELAX and LIGHTEN UP is also a learning process... learning to relax and lighten up which also means learning to be at ease.

Perhaps now, you can imagine yourself at the top of a staircase with ten steps going down. You've been at the top of staircases before, and you will be again. So this is completely familiar to you.

This is a time when you can just put your trust in the world and in the bannister, the handrail that you firmly feel in your dominant hand.

The sun is at your back and when you walk down the stairs you will be going deep, deep asleep for the night. And, you will experience a deep and wonderful sleep, with positive dreams that guide you and lead you to a more wonder tomorrow, and the day after.

You hold on to the bannister and at no time will you ever be out of control in any way. You can trust, just like you did when you were a very, very little person. And everything is going to turn out exactly as you want it to. We're going to walk down these steps together, if you want to, and with every step down you take, you're going to relax just a little bit more.

And now, if you will, you can take the first step down... and you've taken one step down, and you have nine to go. And with every step down, you relax just a little bit more. And any sounds you hear will serve to relax you just a little bit more.

 *And way, way out in the future, and way, way back in the past, and right behind your forehead are those words*

RELAX – LIGHTEN UP

all lit up. And now, you take another step down with me. And you relax just a little bit more, and now you have taken two steps down, and you have eight steps to go....

and take another step down... relaxing a bit more with every step you go down. Feeling that relaxation in your body...you may be surprised at how relaxed you already feel.

and now take another step down, and so far we've gone four steps down and you have six more to go. When you reach the bottom step – you'll enter the door to the sleep room -- Now is the time for relaxation.

It's not important if you go to sleep, but if you want to go through the doorway to sleep, that's fine also. If it happens, that's fine; if your mind drifts away, that's fine. Everything is OK, nothing that you do is wrong.

Take one more step down. You are now halfway down the stairs... and another sign.

RELAX – LIGHTEN UP

You have five more steps to go... and you take another step down. And feel yourself, consciously feel yourself on the sixth step down, and how comfortable you feel, and how secure you feel, and how trusting you feel.

And now one more step down... and now you've taken seven steps down and you have three to go. And there's that word RELAX shining way, way out in your own inner mind, right behind your forehead at the same time... and you take another step down...and you've taken eight steps and you see LIGHTEN UP and you feel much lighter.

And now one more step... and you've taken nine steps down and you have one to go... and now take that last step, and you're all the way down to the bottom of the stairs. And you may be surprised at how relaxed you really are.

And now you see a doorway to sleep, and if you want to, you can go through the door and you enter, and -- you can see yourself on a lovely, lovely, warm, comfortable beach.

Way out in front of you is a calm, calm, very blue ocean, very calm and very blue. See if you can smell what the ocean smells like. Really try to smell it. Be there. And the sun is just gently warming your body in a way that can't hurt you under any circumstances...

Now, you feel the cool breeze over your body and how comfortable that feels to you. You hear the waves of the ocean in the background. Listen to what they sound like. Underneath your feet is the warm sand, just the right temperature, the way you like it best. Behind you is an enormous beach, friendly and protective and just wonderful.

Now, while you're standing there, perhaps you can see yourself as a very, very little person at a time when you were very happy, very content, and very secure. Feel that happiness, and feel that security. Feel that carefree feeling, and know that that's you.

Remember that any noise you hear will just relax you further. And you can recall this feeling of happiness and contentment any time you want to... it's your feeling and it's your memory. You are the only one in the world with this memory.

 *Now, see yourself on the beach once again, as an adult now, knowing that there's a large, comfortable, beach towel on the beach to guard your head from the sand.*

So, just allow yourself to lie down on your back and feel how secure the beach sand is under you, holding your entire body comfortably. Feel how secure that is.

See yourself, surrounded by a white light. It covers every inch of your body while all the normal functions go on. You breathe normally and your mind opens and absorbs the light as if it is the light of the sun, and the light at perfect strength and intensity to make you feel – really, really good.

The normal functions of your body continues, and that white light is a combination of all of the healing energies that exist in this Universe, and all of the healing powers of your own body, and all of the healing power of any medication you're taking or and form of treatment that you are now taking... and that white light can go any area of the body that we ask for it to go. You tell it to.

Now, I want you to see that part of your body that is not exactly as you want it to be and slowly direct that white light to go to that part of your body and surround that area and any other areas simultaneously. Be aware of the white light surrounding your body combines all of the healing forces of the Universe, and all of the healing power in your body and mind, and all of the healing power of any therapies you're current on and any other healing modalities you are using.

It's an extraordinarily powerful elixir. And any cells that are there are weak or weird immediately are healed, or are immediately replaced by new healthy ones. You can direct the white light to heal

 *any area of ityour body to improve your overall health -- and to do anything you want it to do.*

The white light is a powerful, vital, revitalizing and rejuvenating force that totally transforms your health and well-being for the better.

Consciously, you envision the white light surrounding all of the areas where your body is not in the condition you want it to be. And now I want you to notice... notice how the process is bringing in the endorphins of your brain down into that area and soothing any discomforts and alleviating any problem that's going on in your body -- simply tell the white light to do what you want it to do – it is yours. It is going to go where you want it to. And by telling it where you want it to go, you take charge of your body.

Now, I will remain silent for a while, and you will want to see, think, and feel that white light doing all the things you want it to do. I'm going to be quiet starting now.

[pause 60 seconds]

Now, that white light is still within you. That powerful, vigorous, vital white light now is within you. That light combines all of the power of the universe to work in your body. It's totally and completely at your command, now and forever.

Now see yourself standing up on the beach. Visualize yourself without any physical problems whatsoever, no aches, no pains, no problems – you are perfectly healthy. Now, imagine the light healing your thoughts. Notice that white light, you can flip a switch and summon up the power of recall memory.

Each and every time you flip the switch you power up – LIGHTEN UP, you RELAX and LIGHTEN UP and life gets better, better, and better. And your attitude gets better, and better, and better.

And now that you're feeling that white light, you can call on that feeling at any time. You call on that feeling of the white light, or you can call on the feeling of security and protection at any time you desire, without interfering with anything that you're doing.

And now you walk through the door that says SLEEP and you just relax, and lighten up. And you can go deep asleep tonight and have a wonderful peaceful sleep. You go deeper and deeper asleep for the night.

And tomorrow when you awaken, you will feel wonderful at the sight of the Light, daylight, sunrise, dawn, or using your Light Machine. And, now you go deeper, deeper, asleep – down, down into a deep, deep sleep, deep asleep for the night.

Hypnosis & Visualization with Light Source.
A trip to your private Hawaiian Beach (record for playback)

Imagine having your own private beach especially designed for your personal vacation – just to help you relax, reduce or eliminate stress, tension and depression from your entire body and mind. There, you feel the ultimate relaxation experience.

You'll also get to know the ocean and the beach – and experience total freedom from life's responsibilities for a short vacation on your own safe and secluded private beach at this Hawaiian paradise with your own vacation home. Can you imagine this? Just try?

Pretend with the power of your imagination – that you can see it. Imagine it as a small, even half-moon shaped beach, and although there are sailboats, a yacht, and other boats in sight, and even a hot air balloon, in the distance - no feet have ever touched this pristine white sand in a many, many years.

While there, you'll be able to spend some time enjoying your hammock, looking out onto the horizon and seeing the endless sea. Your eyes will be graced by seeing the different spectral colors in your view. The yellow morning sun, the golden setting sun, the blue of the sky and the ocean, the glittering of the sand, the green, red, yellow, orange, purple, and blues of the flowers that surround you at the beach.

At the same time, while you are relaxing in nature -- all your stresses, cares, and worries … just float away -- never to return.

On your own private beach, the sounds of the waves relax you, the view of the ocean and the waves breaking into foam on the shore – relaxes you. The gentle Pacific trade winds that blow also tend to cause you to relax more and more, and you will be always free from worries and concerns.

And in a few moments, I am going to help you to achieve some of the deepest levels of relaxation using your memories from your own experience, memories of movies, photos, or things you've heard of, to create your own personal experience right now of taking a visit to a private beach so that you can detach from the stresses of the day and achieve the deepest level of relaxation so in the future you will be far more focused, and more motivated to have better days.

From this little journey to the beach you will learn how to disappear mental and physical stress and tension, and feel rejuvenated and revitalized, just as if you've had a weekend at the beach. So, let's begin the journey.

Today we are going to travel to a private beach - to a place where the beach itself - is the entire experience - and as you simply can imagine that you are arriving - on your own private plane – a limousine van waiting for you there - to take you - along the tropical beach road - to your private beach. Look at the ocean along the peaceful road. You notice no other car along this road dirt road in a long time. The road looks groomed - and the foliage on the side of the road - appears to be full and yet groomed. You can see the ocean on one side, trees and flowers on the other.

You look towards the ocean – it appears endless. It just merges into the horizon and there isn't a cloud in the sky.

As you watch the flowers, the ocean, nature, and you take it all in … your subconscious mind is in complete control of mind and body and is permitting you to clearly see in your mind's eye what I suggest that you see, and you realize that you are so safe and peaceful here, safe and at peace while relaxing in a light hypnosis trance while you are visiting your beach.

You also know that you can do anything that you set your mind to do - without leaving the peace and serenity of your own private beach.

And now letting your subconscious drift wherever it will as you love the experience of being here and enjoying your massage while being at your own private beach -- and you also know that whenever you want, you can return to this beach and be present to love and enjoy another day of sunslight, sunshine, peacefulness and total and complete relaxation.

As you get closer to the beach, the realization of being here to relax takes over your mind. You realize that you are already relaxing, and letting go off any thoughts other than being

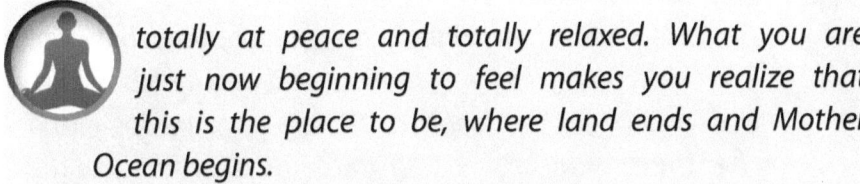

totally at peace and totally relaxed. What you are just now beginning to feel makes you realize that this is the place to be, where land ends and Mother Ocean begins.

Yes - here you can relax, because here there are no phones, no cell towers, no modern mode of communication, no televisions, no bosses, no clients, no responsibilities, no stresses, no worries, and – just one universal being … a oneness - of being at peace -- peace, peace, peace – and being free, and enjoying the here and now, total relaxation -- you are here at your own private place, in paradise.

From the air strip, the van slowly goes down to your tiny Hawaiian beach paradise, which is yours for as long as you desire to be here.

As the van slowly pulls up to the exclusive beach, you realize how quiet it is and you can hear birds singing and the great sound of Mother Ocean as she breaks on the shore into foam and kisses the sand and slowly retreats. You feel the energy of the ocean and she relaxes you.

The driver opens your door, and you notice the humidity, then – you are aware of the tranquility, finally you take in the immenseness of the vista – directly in front of you.

As you look out on the ocean, you see some yachts and sailboats in the distance, and one hot air balloon – but all are very, very, far from your private beach.

Everything is ocean, except for this beach, with its waves rolling in and going out, and rolling in and going out, you draw in a breath of clean, fresh, slightly salty air, through your nostrils, and you realize it's clean air, and you can just take slow deep breaths --- and you relax … deeper and deeper.

And, you can feel the sunlight on your forehead, between your eyes, going deep inside your head, and it feels GOOD. Now you begin to taste the saltiness on your lips – and you feel the air - the breeze, and you sense the totality of the peaceful serenity around you. It begins to permeate every fiber of your being.

As you sit on the beach and soft, warm, sand you notice some round rocks that have been made smooth, which provide hours of fun as you skip them across the surface of the sea, counting how many skips each stone makes on its journey back into the sea.

You decide to walk in and test the water with your bare feet, but you really don't go too far out, just about up to your knees. You feel that the water is warm and salty, and it's a very clean fragrance reminds you that this experience can only be known in the waters of a paradise under the sunshine - you feel peace, at peace with yourself, the world, and everyone in it.

You now go over to a hammock which is strung between two coconut palms. You notice that the hammock has the sign RESERVED and your name under it in fine hand calligraphy. You put the sign aside and you just slide onto the hammock and just relax your body and mind completely, relaxing, deeper and deeper.

This is your place, your space, your peaceful place of serenity, your personal paradise here in your own mind. Here you do experience total and complete relaxation, and peaceful serenity now and whenever you desire to visit in the future.

You look around and see all the lush tropical foliage – beautiful but huge flowers, amazingly tall palm trees, with piles of ripe coconuts on the ground, another pile is ripe pineapples, another is mangos, another pile is fresh lemons, and a huge cooler with ice, and fine bottled waters, and your own private collection of fruit juices, and a private juice bar.

In a moment a fruit drink appears, and you close your eyes as if talking to your own higher power, and just say "Thanks." Yes, life is good.

The sun is high in the sky; you just call for someone to put sun tan lotion on you and you feel someone massaging suntan lotion into your skin.

If it is too warm – simply, mentally call out and someone will fan you with a Rama branch from a coconut palm.

You feel just perfect here and you have all the time in the world just to relax, and enjoy your little piece of paradise.

You have as long or as short a time here to enjoy the sun and fun at the beach, with its calm blue waters and safe and beautiful white waves in the early afternoon sun. You look at the shore and see the contrasting colors of the sun, the beach sand in its tan and glittering appearance as if it were embedded with tiny diamond chips, the ocean with its blue-green majesty and the sky in a perfect shade of blue with a few white clouds, these are the most natural and relaxing things that you can imagine.

Now just lie on your back, and watch a cloud change shape, or make it totally dematerialize right before your eyes. Yes, you are that powerful.

You realize that this beautiful place in nature, this small and private beach was created just the way it is - just for you ... only for you. And, you see those who are attending to you on this beach paradise, smiling because you are happy, content, relaxed, serene, and peaceful – and that makes their jobs so much more rewarding for each of them.

As time goes on here you are much more happy than before. Your happiness meter keeps going up and up and up as you reflect upon about your life, and you see that it can be even happier if you could only pack up all your cares and woes and send them packing. You are taking all your troubles, and all the troubles of the world and packing them in a strong wooden chest, like a pirate's chest ...

'See yourself doing that packing up of all your worries and putting them in this chest until the chest is full ... and you are empty of cares and woes, troubles and fears, doubts and disbeliefs, hurts and pains, sadness and any other non-productive emotions like, envy or jealousy, guilt or shame – pack them all up – pack them and close the lid, put on the lock, and wrap it in chains and locks and test it and it is strong and impenetrable, and watch as you WILL that Hot Air Balloon that you saw earlier, to come to shore and land right next to you. And, as if by magic, your limo-van driver comes to your side and with his muscular build he lifts this chest with all the cares and woes, and puts it is the hot air balloon's basket that normally carries people.

He lights up the gas jet, and slowly adjusts it so that the hot air balloon begins to float away, and the winds of change blow the hot air balloon far, far away - as you celebrate the freedom from worry and stress, cares and fears -- carried away by the winds to another place from whence they can never return, all your problems, troubles, cares, and woes, are all going to where they shall have absolutely no impact upon you or anyone else now, nor ever again.

Now imagine all your troubles floating away in the basket of the hot air balloon, never to return. (30 seconds silence)

As time passes, you gain more confidence, as you realize that you can take all your troubles, and all the troubles of the world and

 *have them fly away, as if carries by the winds of time to another place in time, where they have no impact upon you or anyone else now, or in the future.*

As the sun sets, it's cooler and you feel relaxed. You realize that life is good, you know it, and you are thinking more clearly now. You can sense things from other viewpoints; you seem to be able to be detached from reality when you relax in this way, and later you awaken and maintain a great deal of inner peace when you return to your real world.

From now on, you can see things from an unemotionally detached viewpoint like a bird flying overhead. You sense the same feeling of being able to soar – the feeling of being free - you imagine that you are the bird and you are soaring ever higher and higher and feeling the sun shining on you.

And, at the same moment, from this detached viewpoint, you can see yourself below, peaceful here on your own private beach.

Now draw in another deep breath, and anchor this entire beach experience to sound of the ocean – each and every time you think of the ocean, you are as deeply relaxed and at peace as you are right now. The thought of the ocean, the sound of the ocean all make you relax and relax and relax more and more.

And as of now you remain calm and relaxed. You have greater confidence, inner strength, and you accept yourself as you are. Yes, you respect yourself, you accept and respect yourself, and with that inner foundation of self-love and love for life, you are empowered to greatness in your life. And, more than that, you are beginning to feel happier, and happier every day. You see the humor in life, you see the humor in life - and you smile, you grim, you laugh.

You notice – that all of your past tensions have already been packaged up and taped closed, and wrapped with chains and locks, and sent to flight in the basket of a hot air balloon that will carry those worries, past memories, and any hurts – out, out, out past the horizon, and you totally released them, and from now on – whenever you feel stress or tension - you just pack it up, and set the hot air balloon to float off, off, off, past the horizon – and you just let go off tension and worry, and you still go deeper and deeper. And you are laughing at how easy it was to get rid of it all, and become happier, and happier, and happier.

And as you relax you review your life for anything that might be limiting you from having the best possible successes, and enjoying happiness at every turn. And you just, send them off to catch the hot air balloon, and all that remains is happiness and the most awesome levels of inner peace. All because you have released any beliefs that restricted you from achieving everything you want. You just sent the thoughts to the hot air balloon and blew them away to a point that you have no self-limiting beliefs.

As a seagull is looking down on the earth, you can see in great detail … the hammock, the mini-van, the driver, and the others who will serve you. And just beyond the hammock is a path to your beach home that you will be relaxing and enjoying time at … later.

You open your eyes from being entranced by nature and pleasant thought, and you are escorted to your home, where you will be treated to relaxing music, massage to fortify your body and your just cleansed spirit and to increase your sense of your having a healthy body and mind, normal and healthy peaceful sleep, and a path towards excellence in every way.

Your home is a combination of wood, brick, and glass, and it is very well constructed with an angled roof covered with Ramas: dried leaves and branches from the coconut palm. With its modern and traditional style all in one, there is an exposed deck to the beach

 *and ocean through open sliding glass doors onto a large open sundeck downstairs with the most comfortable chair imaginable and another floor upstairs.*

Here your personal massage therapist is ready to complete today's massage from your upper deck with a beautiful and relaxing view of the pristine sands, the ocean, the waves, the horizon, the setting sun, and you realize – all too soon, that soon the massage will be over, so for now you just feel it, experience, let it go, let it flow, let it happen, total release, total peacefulness – total freedom - total happiness.

You sense all of this in your own mind, very clearly, and exactly the way that is most pleasing to you - and you have seen it internally through your ability to visualize, to detach from reality and fly like a seagull and get an overview of your own special world – your private beach.

And in a little while, your driver will take you back in the mini-van to your plane and back to your real world.

Later, upon awakening, you will recall all the wonderful feelings that you have experienced at the beach, and you know that you have the clarity and power to be happy, healthy, and more alive with life energy than you have ever, ever been before.

From this moment on you feel revitalized, energized, and inspired simply because you have the ability to return to your private beach every single day, so that you can re-experience your time of peace and serenity at any time that you desire to do so.

And any time you want to recall these wonderful memories, all you have to do is to take a very deep breath, and just think about the ocean at your beach and the experience it will all come flooding back, a beautiful day of just you, on your beach.

And now your driver helps you with your things, and you get into the mini-van, take a last look at your own personal paradise and feel the warmth of the sunshine, and you promise yourself to return very soon. The driver now begins to drive back to your plane which will take you home.

And when you awaken you in a few moments time, you will feel as though you have been to the beach for a day trip. You will feel happy and content and ready to face any of life's little challenges feeling clear, calm, peace, happy, and empowered. And so it is!

Hypnosis & Visualization with Light Source in the Morning. A trip to the Beach (record for playback)

And, now relax, get into a comfortable position, put your hands in the mudra meditation pose, and draw in a very, very, deep, deep breath. In-in-in and hold it for a few seconds. Now, slowly relax and exhale.

Make sure that your Light Box is illuminated, and close your eyes, and imagine now the most beautiful summer day. The sky is a perfect blue the sun is shining down on your body.

And, now relax more, keeping your hands in the mudra meditation position, and draw in another very, very, deep, deep breath. In-in-in- and hold it. Slowly relax and exhale. And, one more deep breath, in-in-in and hold it. Slowly relax and begin to imagine that you are outside - perhaps imagine you are at a beautiful beach, where on the way there, there are many sweet scented flowers and fruit trees, oranges, lemons, mangos, along the way.

 *Imagine the scent of your favorite flowers - breathe it in - and relax - and feel the sun on your body - warming you gently all over.*

Listen to the songs of the birds in the trees - become at one with nature and all her beauty.

Notice the color of the leaves on the trees - so many different shades of green, it's the end of spring, almost summer here.

And feel the sensation of a very gentle breeze - blowing from time time on your skin and on your hair.

To your left is a pond with wildlife visiting throughout the year just to sip water and chew on the long pond grass.

In spring and summer the place is alive with singing birds of all kinds which stop, drink, and continue on their journeys.

As well as birds - dragonflies are flying around the lake - on warm summer days like today, you can see them from the shore.

Beyond the pond is flower-filled fields and butterflies. Enjoy this wonderful view - see how good it makes you feel.

You walk down a path that goes to a small hill that leads to an old abandoned chapel. The kind that big ranches sometimes have so that people can go nearby to pray.

It's very peaceful up here - and you look around for a comfortable place to sit and rest, and be at peace in the front of the chapel. Although there is no place to be comfortable outside the chapel, you do have the most fantastic view of the pond, the fields with wildflowers and trees and a little stream that goes through the nearby woods.

And as you walk into the chapel and sit down on an old fashioned pew, you look at the light beaming through the stained glass windows, and the light points to a spot on a bench - you just go over there to the bench, and on the exact spot where the sun hits the bench, you place your head, face up, so that the light shines on the space between your eyes, your forehead. Your mind's eye is now getting the sunlight treatment. And, now you allow your eyes to gently close as you feel the warming sunlight on your brow - this makes you feel good - it makes you feel so calm, happy - and at peace with yourself, the world, and everyone in it.

As you begin to drift deeper and deeper you begin to imagine yourself on a journey within yourself. You're standing at the bottom of a stairway leading up to your brain's higher control center. You ascend higher and higher, feeling lighter and lighter as you seem to float up each step, as if you feel like you are walking on air. You feel so light, comfortable, and relaxed.

At the top of the stairway is a door - with a sign BRAIN - Higher Control Center - and you open the door and walk in. You begin to look around - and you can see the inside of your head - looking up just inside the forehead - you notice a gland - it's your pineal gland - your third eye. Yes, the human body has another physical eye whose function has long been recognized by humanity.

It is called the 'Third Eye' or 'Mind's Eye' which in reality is the Pineal Gland. It is long thought to have quite amazing powers. Many consider it our Inner Vision.

Your Pineal Gland is about the size of a sweet pea, located in the centre of the brain above the pituitary gland which lies a little behind the root of the nose. It is located right behind the eyes.

The true function of the Pineal is still unknown but mystics and philosphers agree that it is very powerful. Ancient Greeks believed *the pineal gland to be our connection to the world of Thought. Descartes called it the Seat of the Soul.*

The Pineal is activated by Light, and it works in harmony with the hypothalamus gland which directs the body's thirst, hunger, sexual desire and the biological clock that determines our aging process.

When the pineal gland wakes up you can feel a little pressure at the base of the brain. It's pleasurable and often occurs when you connect to a higher frequency.

I'm going to show you a way to overcome those old feelings of yours - to bring yourself back to this more happy and pleasurable state of mind while relaxing in your favorite place of serenity.

In your higher mind - I want you to visualize a perfect diamond - and in the centre of this diamond is your pineal gland.

Remember it's shape, like a pea - and it's function, thought, emotions, appetite, - and bring to mind an image of many type of flourescent light units to shine over each and every facet of the diamond. Where the interse light can focus on your pineal gland, creating that slight pleasurable pressure at the base of your brain. You are connecting to that higher frequency, and the amount of melatonin secreted by your gland is now reduce for the rest of the day.

From now on you use your Light box and your hypnosis audios every single day, and by spending the time with hypnosis, and going through this process you feel better, better, and better. You sense your life taking a turn, a turn for the better. You are happier, more motivated, and driven to be successful. You use your Light Box, Your Hypnosis, your meditation and you are a much happier person. And as you do - you're amazed at how much better you

 *feel. You have more energy - more aliveness - and your mood is happier and you feel just great.*

And every day - especially in winter - you make it your committment to spend at least one hour a day in natural sunlight and using your Light Box to help you feel better. You are now enjoying the fresh air and appreciating each season as it comes and goes. You also setup your office and home to be more open to receiving natural sunlight, and using special lighting where there is no sunlight access. And every day you feel better and happier - you have more energy - much more energy. You feel fantastic and are at peace with yourself, the world, and everyone in it.

In a moment I'm going to count from one to five and at the count of five you'll be wide awake, and you'll feel alive with life, ready to begin your day, you feel as if you've had 8 hours of wonderfully relaxing sleep and now you are ready to face the day, happy, healthy, alive with live. And as each day passes each suggestion I've given to you becomes TWICE as effective as it was the day before.

Coming up now, slowly -

1. *you feel good all over - positive and confident, alive with live.*

2. *you are positive and happy, you feel that life is good, and it is good.*

3. *you are a winner, positive, happy, confident, and alive with life - coming up a little more*

4. *almost there, almost there, and on the next number you'll be wide -wide awake*

5. *number 5 - and you are wide, wide awake.*

STEP 7:
The Magical Secret
to Being Happy

ABOUT HAPPINESS

Where Are You Now?
Where Do You Want to Be?

I remember a trip I took, it was about 6 years ago. I asked my good buddy Dan, an engineer, to drive me to a city about an hour away so we could get things at Costco and get some great Chinese food.

I sent him an email with the town name, and got a return email with the latitude and longitude for his GPS (Global Positioning System). When he arrived he had his GPS turned on, like those available for nearly all vehicles today, connected to his laptop (yeah, these were the old days), and he was marking points we traveled in that City for easy recall later by the GPS.

What took place is that he placed a small antenna on his car's windshield to send a signal to a satellite, somewhere floating in space, which identified his antenna's location. (This is very ancient technology today, but you'll get the point.)

Once he entered the coordinates:

FROM--->   **TO**
(his current position)   *(desired destination)*

The GPS calculated the best route between where we were and where we wanted to go. The screen showed him the distance that we must travel. It also recommended the best routes for him to get us there. It also showed current detours and barriers. It was amazing.

With today's technology, the GPS will give you by spoken word the specific directions necessary to get you to your destination at convenient reminders like turn left 100 feet ahead. Soon they will have ones that say "Stop quickly! Barely-conscious human being crossing against the light."

If life, itself, were just that easy, with a GPS in control you would never lose your North – you'd know exactly where you were at every moment. And…

The great thing about the GPS is that it doesn't ask you: "Where were you?" It does not ask: "Why were you there so long?" and a million other questions that could take you off course in life like "Who were you with?" and "What were you doing with THAT PERSON for so long?

The GPS has only one purpose -- to help you to get from point A to point B; from where you are -- to where you want to be.

Your feelings work to provide a similar system to guide you. Their primary function is to help you travel the distance from where you are -- to where you want to be.

It is important to know WHERE YOU ARE in relationship to WHERE YOU WANT TO BE. Knowing this, you'll get closer to where you want to be. If you want to make intentional decisions, you must know where you are and where you are going to, in other words – you must have your own point A (starting point) point B (destination) and any stops in between or a point C (a further destination). You must know where you are going.

We're surrounded by many influences in our environments. Sometimes others ask, or demand of us, that we behave differently. This is to give THEM a more positive experience of knowing us. Generally, we tend to be flooded with laws, rules, and expectations imposed by others. Everyone has an opinion about what we should do, be, or have, and a whole bunch more like how we should feel. People keep shoulding on us and realistically we can't stay on track between where we are and where we want to be, if outside influences are always playing back seat driver, screwing up our travel plans.

Sometimes we are pulled this way or that way trying to please others. And then we discover that no matter how hard we try, we cannot consistently move in any positive direction. We not only do not please others, we do not please ourselves either. We get pulled in so many different directions at once, our path to the direction where we want to be, our destination, usually gets lost in the process. TURN ON YOUR GPS FAST!

Your Greatest Gift To Give To Others Is Your Happiness.

The greatest gift that you could ever give to another is for them to experience your happiness. When you are experiencing joy, happiness, or appreciation, you are fully connected to the stream of pure, positive Source (God) energy that we spoke about earlier -- the energy of your true self. When you are in that state of connection, anything or anyone that you are focusing on, benefits from your attention.

APPRECIATION

Thought is Energy. Positive thought is high energy, negative thoughts or fears are low energies.

Appreciation is HIGH ENERGY. It is very similar to love, the highest of energies. The vibration of appreciation is very high indeed and is very positive towards empowerment. While we are in a state of appreciating, we tend to be in perfect harmony with the Creative Source, God.

So be more appreciative. I've heard that every time you are in thankfulness and appreciation mode, you are hundreds of times more effective than in any other mode. That sounds great to me.

Find something to be thankful for and work with that energy. Use that energy to feel and then visualize the positive transference of that energy of successful thankfulness towards your new goal.

Visiting foreign countries is something I love to do. I appreciate the people, the architecture, the culture and many other things. Going to 3rd world countries gives you other things to be thankful for. Wherever I travel, when I go to a pharmacy which now seems to be a mini-supermarket, I go to the candy section and wherever I can find a Peter Paul ALMOND JOY in the midst of all the different varieties of local brands of candy, chocolate, and flavors from elsewhere nearby, I am very appreciative of the ALMOND JOY and always buy a few to keep my appreciation level high.

Childhood favorite snacks can quickly elevate your appreciation. By the way, does anyone know where I can buy Good 'n Plenty in Latin America where I am writing this from?

I think that Good n' Plenty would sure go a long way with mental programming. Just think a positive or wonderful thought, like how good your vacation in Cancun was last year, and chew up a Good n' Plenty candy just to anchor that feeling that it was Good n' you want Plenty more of those thoughts and those vacations.

It's a great anchor for happiness- think a happy thought, and anchor it with one Good n' Plenty candy. The key is ONE Good n' Plenty candy can become your magic pill to reinforce a positive thought to make it more likely to occur again.

Other things can be used for appreciation anchoring: A great movie, a good hug, a great Chinese buffet once a month, your child's birthday party, seeing your mother-in-law go home, and after that a night of great lovemaking.

Give thanks and appreciate everything you have in life.

There is NO ONE else who needs you -- to be, or to do things for them, in order for them to feel happy. Everyone has the same access to this stream of consciousness that you do. Others, who can't understand having this access, suffer because they can't keep a feel-good attitude. They sometimes demand that you behave in a way that they think will make them feel better. **<u>Don't do it</u>**!

Not only do they make you a doormat for their joy, they place themselves as slaves to their own sick situation. They will never be able to control the way other people behave. And, if controlling others is necessary for their happiness, they are in serious trouble themselves.

Your Happiness Does Not Depend on What Others Do. Your happiness does not depend on others. It all depends on your own vibrational energy. Another's happiness cannot depend on you, but on his or her vibration. The way anyone feels at any moment, is only about their own energy situation. The way you feel is an indication of the vibrating energy balance between your desires and your personal feeling (vibes). These have been launched into action.

Happiness is really about choice. The more happiness you choose, the more life presents you with experiences to feel happy with. If you are feeling blue or even downright depressed, you must make the decision to "forget your troubles, come on get happy."

AN OLD MYTH: "I will be happy when..."

What do you think would truly make you happy? Let's suppose one of your answers would be to have more money. If you were given a billion dollars but told that you couldn't spend any of it, money would do you no good. If you were given a house that no one could ever live in, you would find that house worthless, too.

Or, is it "I will be happy when: I find a boyfriend, get engaged, get married, go on my honeymoon, have my first baby, when my child goes to school, when I stop having these danged kids, when the kids are grown up, when my kids are married, when my husband retires, when we go on vacation, when I have my first grandchild..." You are missing a lot of life this way. Why don't you just be happy HERE and NOW?

So, tell me what you want, what you really, really want? What do you really want? If you don't know, you'll greedily pursue material things, thinking they will satisfy your happiness needs. Whatever you desire is abundantly available and is not limited to the resources of the physical world.

Experiencing Love is all you really want and need. Money, treasures, even good health and better relationships may be things you think you need. But, they are only a strategy of this temporary, forever changing, physical world we live in. Perhaps they are important in this dimension, but when you are totally awakened by spiritual Love, you'll realize you don't need anything else.

Where are you looking for Love, all the wrong places, no doubt. True Love, like true happiness, is abundantly available and comes from within you. Not at some bar!

It doesn't mean you can't work at a great job, have better health, or enjoy a yacht and a multi-million dollar home. These are for you to enjoy while you are here on the planet. Once you've awakened to being a spiritual being, you'll freely experience all of life's rewards, in addition to simply being alive. You'll no longer believe you 'need' anything to find happiness. You may say, "Yes, but love doesn't pay the bills."

Survival is important, but surviving is not our purpose here. We're here to enjoy and love this experience on earth -- and remember who we are.

The Greatest Secret To Happiness

We become happiest by broadening our horizon beyond our own selves. From research related to anxiety and depression we know that being unhappy and depressed are extremely self-focused, or selfish states of being. This will tend to upset many people, but when they think and analyze it ... it's true.

However, during periods of inner stress or unhappiness, if we do something for someone else, that state of self-focus immediately dissolves. If you were to think of any time that you had a down feeling, and then a friend or relative phoned and screamed "help, I'm in trouble and I need help now." Immediately your focus shifted to being a helper to a friend in need.

You stopped feeling blue because you gained the energy ... and right away – you may have even felt better, and helping another helped you gain some proper perspective on what was going on with you.

Being Compassionate Makes You Attractive

Above everything else in life the most desired thing that people want is love. We look for it everywhere. At work, we want recognition. At home, we want respect, and loving kindness. In our loving relationship – we want love in the form of closeness. Basically, we want great relationships and we want to be liked.

When we seek to be loved by others, we sometimes will go to any lengths – to gain their attention (including dressing to kill, makeup, even plastic surgery, botox, and the like if we feel insecure about how we feel, and we put on a show or mask/facade to try to gain others attention and then impress them.

This is all to conceal our fragility and how we vulnerable feel. Yes, all of us have great acting abilities when it's needed to impress others.

Being compassionate naturally makes you feel more relaxed and at peace, and happy, all of which will make you look naturally younger and more attractive. This will draw more attention to you.

Compassion Gives You Money and Time

In addition to happiness and love, we all want more time and money. When we do compassionate things, we feel as if time expands. When we give some of our money to others, we sense that we are wealthier, that we have abundance in our lives.

Those who have helped others know that satisfying and fulfilling feeling that follows – that's happiness, beyond the financial reward of any transaction in business or any financial reward.

It is on another level of well-being altogether, just how satisfying and fulfilling that experience can be.

Compassion Boosts Your Health

Research suggests that making a connection with others in a meaningful way helps us better relate and improves our mental and physical health, speeds up recovery from disease and research has shown that it may even lengthen our life. Why does compassion lead to health benefits?

A clue rests in a study that evaluated levels of inflammation at the cellular level in people that describe themselves as "very happy." Now, we all know that a form of inflammation is at the root of cancer and other diseases and is generally high in people who live under a lot of stress.

We might expect that inflammation is lower for people with higher levels of happiness. But, researched determined that this was only the case for certain "very happy" people.

They discovered that people who were happy because they lived the "good life" (sometimes also know as "hedonic happiness") had high inflammation levels but, on the other hand, people who were happy because they lived a life of purpose or meaning had low inflammation levels.

Having a life of meaning and purpose is a life that is focused less on satisfying oneself and more on helping others. It is a life rich in compassion, altruism and greater meaning.

Compassion Uplifts & Spreads

Why are the lives of people like Mother Teresa, Martin Luther King, Pope John Paul II, Desmond Tutu, John F. Kennedy, and others are so inspiring?

It's likely that seeing someone helping another creates a state of what's called "elevation."

Have you ever been moved to tears by seeing someone's loving and compassionate behavior? Elevation inspires us to help others -- and it may just be the force behind giving.

Helping is contagious -- generosity and kindness bring more generosity from others in the form of goodness. You may have seen one of the news reports about chain reactions that occur when someone pays for the toll of the drivers behind them at a at a tollbooth.

In different parts of the country, people demonstrate generosity for hours. Your compassion uplifts others making them happier. By uplifting others you also help yourself.

Further more it's been shown that if the people around us are happy, we, in turn become happier as well.

Compassion is 100% Natural

One reason why compassion might feel so good is that it's natural to us. Research indicates that both humans and animals are loving, generous and kind.

What can we learn from this? Material things may give us fun or short-term pleasure, but long-term happiness and fulfillment lies less in what we can give to others rather than what we can get.

Compassion may just be the best kept secret to being not just happy but also healthy, wealthy, and wise.

Givers gain ...
and takers lose.

WHAT WOULD YOU ATTEMPT IF YOU KNEW YOU COULD NOT FAIL?

www.ingramcontent.com/pod-product-compliance
Lightning Source LLC
Chambersburg PA
CBHW020536290526
45786CB00002B/910